The Couple's DISEASE

Finding a Cure for Your "Lost" Love Life

The Couple's DISEASE

Finding a Cure for Your "Lost" Love Life

Lawrence S. Hakim, MD, FACS

with Donald Michael Platt

Foreword by Irwin Goldstein, MD
Professor of Urology, Boston University School of Medicine

DHP Publishers
Delray Beach, 2002

Copyright © 2002 by DHP Publishers, LLC

Published by DHP Publishers, LLC
1730 S. Federal Highway, Suite #378
Delray Beach, Florida 33483-3309

ISBN #: 0-9710455-0-X

Library of Congress Cataloging-in-Publication Data

Hakim, Lawrence.
  The couple's disease : finding a cure for your "lost" love life /
Lawrence Hakim, with Donald Platt.
      p. cm.
  ISBN 0-9710455-0-X
  1. Sexual disorders—Popular works. I. Platt, Donald. II. Title.
  RC556 .H34 2002
  616.85'83—dc21
                                    2001007516

For Carl DeSantis,
whose encouragement and support
made this book possible.

Contents

	Acknowledgements	xi
	Foreword	xvii
1.	*Communication Interruptus*	*xxiii*
	Introduction	xxv

PART I: A *COUPLE'S* DISEASE | | **1**
2.	*Worse than Cancer?*	*3*
ONE	*Vive La Difference!*	7
TWO	You Are Not Alone	11
3.	*Dr. Hakim's Waiting Room*	*16*
THREE	Believe Them: Validated Studies That Prove You Are Not Alone	17
FOUR	Should We Believe Everything We Are Told?	20
FIVE	What About The Rest Of The World?	24
4.	*Dr. Hakim's Waiting Room*	*28*
SIX	Communicate, Communicate, Communicate!	29
SEVEN	Sex, Religion, And Myths	34

PART II: FEMALE SEXUAL RESPONSE | | **41**
5.	*Outside the Clinic*	*43*
EIGHT	Understanding Female Anatomy	44
NINE	Characteristics Of The Female Sexual Response	48
TEN	Stages Of The Female Sexual Response	53
ELEVEN	Cultural Influences	57

PART III: CAUSES OF FEMALE SEXUAL DYSFUNCTION   **59**

TWELVE	Categories Of FSD	61
6.	*Dr. Hakim's Waiting Room*	*67*
THIRTEEN	Pregnancy, Childbirth, Menopause and Hormonal Imbalances	69
7.	*Dr. Hakim's Waiting Room*	*72*
FOURTEEN	Illness And Injury	74
FIFTEEN	Aging	77
8.	*Dr. Hakim's Waiting Room*	*79*
SIXTEEN	Depression	81
9.	*Dr. Hakim's Waiting Room*	*83*
SEVENTEEN	Vaginal Pain	85
EIGHTEEN	Cancer and FSD	88
10.	*Dr. Hakim's Waiting Room*	*91*
NINETEEN	Surgically Induced Menopause	92
TWENTY	Androgens And Estrogens	96

PART IV: MANAGEMENT OF FEMALE SEXUAL DYSFUNCTION   **105**

TWENTY-ONE	Taking The First Step	107
TWENTY-TWO	The Role Of Diagnostic Questionnaires And Medical Histories	111
11.	*Dr. Hakim's Waiting Room*	*115*
TWENTY-THREE	The Physical Exam And Lab Tests	117
TWENTY-FOUR	The Role Of Sexual Therapy	125
TWENTY-FIVE	Will It Also Work For Women?	133
TWENTY-SIX	Estrogen Replacement Therapy	136
TWENTY-SEVEN	Androgen Insufficiency Syndrome And Androgen Replacement Therapy	139
12.	*Dr. Hakim's Office*	*142*
TWENTY-EIGHT	The Magic Pill	144
13.	*Dr. Hakim's Waiting Room*	*151*
TWENTY-NINE	FDA Approved	153

THIRTY	In The Future For Women	156
14.	*Dr. Hakim's Office*	*158*

PART V: MALE ERECTILE DYSFUNCTION   **161**

THIRTY-ONE	Of International Concern	163
THIRTY-TWO	Man's Other Brain	165
THIRTY-THREE	What Causes ED	170
THIRTY-FOUR	Lifestyle Issues	175
15.	*Dr. Hakim's Examining Room*	*178*
THIRTY-FIVE	Vasculogenic And Neurogenic ED	180
THIRTY-SIX	Andropause	184
THIRTY-SEVEN	Drugs And Medications	187
16.	*Dr. Hakim's Waiting Room*	*190*
THIRTY-EIGHT	Physical Trauma	192
THIRTY-NINE	Aging, Other Systemic Diseases, And Prostate Cancer	194
FORTY	More Than "Just Cough And Turn Your Head!"	199
17.	*Dr. Hakim's Examining Room*	*204*
FORTY-ONE	Oral Non-Hormonal Treatment Of ED	229
18.	*Dr. Hakim's Waiting Room*	*213*
FORTY-TWO	Hormone Replacement Therapy	215
FORTY-THREE	Vacuum Erection Devices	217
FORTY-FOUR	Self-injection Therapy	219
19.	*Dr. Hakim's Waiting Room*	*223*
FORTY-FIVE	Fixing The Problem: The Role Of Penile Prostheses	225
20.	*Dr. Hakim's Waiting Room*	*233*
FORTY-SIX	Microvascular Arterial Bypass Surgery	235
FORTY-SEVEN	Premature Ejaculation	238
FORTY-EIGHT	Priapism	241
21.	*Dr. Hakim's Waiting Room*	*243*
FORTY-NINE	Peyronie's Disease	245

22.	*Dr. Hakim's Office*	*250*
FIFTY	If Looks Could Thrill! Phalloplasty And Penile Cosmetic Surgery	252

PART VI: COMPLEMENTARY AND ALTERNATIVE MEDICINE AND SEXUAL FUNCTION **259**

FIFTY-ONE	Herbals And Other Alternate Therapies	261
FIFTY-TWO	Aphrodisiacs And Dangerous Herbals	264
FIFTY-THREE	Nutritional Supplements, Validated Studies, And Female Sexual Function	271
FIFTY-FOUR	Herbals And MED	277

PART VII: PRESCRIPTION FOR SEXUAL HEALTH **279**

23.	*Dr. Hakim's Office*	*281*
FIFTY-FIVE	I.N.T.I.M.A.C.Y.™ My 8-Step Couple's Relationship Enhancement Program	283
24.	*Dr. Hakim's Office*	*298*

APPENDIX A: SEXUALLY TRANSMITTED DISEASES	299
APPENDIX B: HELPFUL ORGANIZATIONS	309
APPENDIX C: RECOMMENDED READING	311

Acknowledgments

The writing of this book has been an incredible learning experience for me, and I have come to realize that an undertaking such as this does not happen overnight, or without significant help and support from many people.

First and foremost, I want to thank Carl DeSantis for his wonderful friendship, incredible generosity and never-ending encouragement. You have taught me a great deal about life and people, about reaching your potential and being successful, and about the true gift of "giving". For that, I am eternally indebted. You are indeed one of a kind and a very special human being.

I want to thank all of my patients and their partners over the years whom I have had the privilege to care for, who have taught me and offered their insight and an opportunity to improve their lives; you truly motivated me to write this book. To those who have given me the gift of their time as I wrote this book, I am especially grateful. I sincerely hope that this book will help many people to reach greater sexual satisfaction, enhanced intimacy and the happiness that so many couples have told me I helped them achieve.

I would like to mention my indebtedness to the amazing teachers and colleagues I have been fortunate to work with throughout my career, all of whom have in some part enabled me to reach this point. Dr. Richard J. Macchia,

Chairman of Urology at SUNY Brooklyn, Dr. Aizid Hashmat and Dr. Richard (Doc) Fairbanks; you helped guide me and opened the doors to my future. Dr. Robert Krane, who passed away during the writing of this book, thanks for your wonderful kindness, support and humor. I want to express my sincere thanks to Dr. Ajay Nehra of the Mayo Clinic for his support and friendship and include my friends and colleagues at the University of Miami, especially Dr. Ray Leveillee for his humor and friendship, Dr. Norman Block for his wisdom and those great Friday night stories, Dr. Victor Politano and Dr. Hernan Carrion for your unselfish guidance and support.

I want to express thanks to my colleagues and friends at the Cleveland Clinic, the premier medical center in the world. Though too numerous to include all by name, I want to particularly mention Dr. Lee Jackson, Dr. Danny Shoskes, Dr. Gamal Ghoniem, Dr. Robert Kay, Dr. Drogo Montague, Dr. Andrew Novick, Dr. Steve Wexner, Dr. Harry Moon, Dr. Juan Nogueras, Mike Albert and Maureen Michaels for your constant support, encouragement and friendship.

My gratitude goes to Donald Michael Platt, a gifted creative writer and a true gentleman, with whom it was a genuine pleasure to work with. A few years ago, when I first conceived of the idea for *The Couple's Disease*, I knew that while medical texts abound, there was a critical need for non-physicians to have a book on female and male sexual health that would not only be informative and comprehensive, but one that would be easily "readable" and able to be enjoyed by all. Donald, with your invaluable assistance and expertise, I feel that we have certainly achieved that lofty goal.

I want to especially thank Dr. Blanche Freund, a wonderful psychologist, sex therapist and friend, for your dedication to our patients and for taking time from your busy work schedule to offer invaluable advice and criticisms during the writing of this book.

I want to thank the many friends who spent their own valuable time proofreading the manuscript, offering constructive criticisms and making useful suggestions. While the list is long, I especially want to mention Ellen Platt, Jim Steinhauser, Gerald Kay and Jack DeNiro for their input during the writing of this book.

I want to acknowledge my parents, Selwyn and Alice Hakim, who have been amazing role models in my life and who taught me important lessons in perseverance, happiness and family. My love to both of you always, for giving me the insight, aspirations and opportunities to succeed.

I want to express my deepest gratitude to my mentor and friend, Dr. Irwin Goldstein, who contributed the *Foreword* to this book. In his autobiography, President George Bush wrote "our lives have defining moments ... that forever change you ... that set you on a different course. Moments of recognition so vivid and so clear that everything later seems different ..." Irwin, meeting you was that defining moment in my life. From those early days in Boston where my training began, you took me under your wing and gave me your gift of enthusiasm and passion for this wonderful and exciting field of female and male sexual dysfunction. You taught me that SD truly is a *couple's* disease, and that no matter how much we think we understand, there are always more questions to be answered. You sir, are truly an outstanding teacher and an inspiration to us all and I will always be grateful for your wisdom, compassion and friendship. I never forgot your words to me when I first began my training with you..."Larry, you were *born* to do this..."

Finally, I want to express my special appreciation to my beautiful family; my wife Elisa, and daughters Ashley and Brittany. Elisa and I, from our school days to the present, have met every new challenge and opportunity together, and the writing of this book was no different. Through the endless days and nights involved in the research, preparation and writing of this book, your immeasurable love kept our family close and allowed our dreams to be reached. You are truly my great love and friend, my sunshine and my inspiration. Your never-ending support continues to guide me and encourage me to achieve even loftier goals than I ever could have imagined. I love you more than you can ever know.

—*Lawrence S. Hakim*

QUESTION: What event takes place more than 100-million times each day worldwide according to the World Health Organization?

ANSWER: Sexual Intercourse!

◆ ◆ ◆

Sexual Health is a Fundamental Right

"There exist fundamental rights for the individual, including the right to sexual health and a capacity to enjoy and control sexual and reproductive behavior in accordance with a social personal ethic — freedom from fear, shame, guilt, false beliefs, and other factors inhibiting sexual response and impairing sexual relationships — freedom from organic disorders, disease, and deficiencies that interfere with sexual and reproductive function."

—*World Health Organization 1994*

Foreword

By Irwin Goldstein, MD
Professor of Urology, Boston University School of Medicine

Over the last several decades, the subspecialty of sexual dysfunction has undergone enormous advancement. Although progress has been especially striking in the basic science research on male erectile dysfunction, its diagnosis and treatment, the focus has now shifted to include research on Female Sexual Dysfunction. *The Couple's Disease* offers the general reader a simplified, yet comprehensive explanation of the current findings, both from the laboratory and the examining room.

Medical techniques employed to male sexual dysfunction have been used as stepping stones to help us understand, diagnose and treat Female Sexual Dysfunction. Although the mechanisms and treatments are different, FSD affects the partners of women with sexual issues as much as impotence affects the partners of men suffering from that dysfunction. It is important to include the partner at every stage of the diagnosis and treatment of female sexual dysfunction, and Dr. Lawrence S. Hakim shows that convincingly in *The Couple's Disease*.

What is so wonderfully distinctive and readable about this book's presentation is the engaging narrative taking place in Dr. Hakim's waiting room, interweaving one couple's story throughout the book with other characters. Text provides background material to help the reader understand what Elizabeth and Brad and the other characters are going through as well as vignettes portraying patients with whom we all can identify.

Part I debunks some of the mysteries around sexual dysfunction. It is not a unique condition; it affects more than 40% of *all* women. Female sexual dysfunction can often be cured, and sometimes prevented. To better understand this, Parts II and III provide the reader with an excellent introduction to female anatomy, which is presented in an understandable way, attempting to simplify the female sexual response. Information on the neural, vascular, hormonal and psychological factors involved in the female sexual response, the current classification system of female sexual dysfunction, along with descriptions of physiological and psychological causes of FSD are treated in close detail with excellent illustrations.

Part IV offers a look at some of the current diagnostic tools and innovative therapies being developed in this emerging field. The step-by-step approach to the management of female sexual dysfunction presented here lets the reader know exactly what to expect from her healthcare specialist.

An underlying and refreshing theme of *The Couples Disease* is that an accurate diagnosis and effective treatment of sexual dysfunction often requires the assistance of professionals from more than one discipline, who can provide treatment from different perspectives. As in all developing fields, additional data is needed to determine the safety and efficacy of all of the treatments. Large scale multi-institutional, placebo controlled, double-blind studies remain to be performed. The safety and efficacy of hormonal treatments in special populations such as pregnant women or those with breast cancer have not been established.

As Dr. Hakim clearly emphasizes in *The Couple's Disease*, it is strongly recommended not to start any treatment, especially hormonal with its concomitant systemic manifestations, without being under the care of a healthcare specialist. Part IV concludes with a look to the future alternatives for women with sexual dysfunction.

Part V is a description of male erectile dysfunction, its causes and therapies, to balance information provided in this book on female sexual dysfunction. Men as well as their partners reading this book together will find a useful discussion including all of the medical and lifestyle issues causing sexual dysfunction in men, such as various systemic risk factors, smoking, medications, surgery and trauma.

As is made clear in *The Couple's Disease*, there is no *single* treatment option that is right for every patient or couple. Dr. Hakim presents detailed descriptions of the actual treatment alternatives available today, ranging from simple lifestyle changes, to various drugs, medical devices and surgical alternatives, with accompanying easy to understand illustrations. Peyronie's disease, priapism and augmentation phalloplasty are also discussed in a detailed and informative manner.

In the 21st century, increasing numbers of couples are turning to Alternative Medicine for answers to improving their lives and health. Part VI looks at the role of Complementary and Alternative Medicine in the treatment of couples with sexual problems. This extremely informative section of the book includes a detailed description of the various herbals, alternative medications and nutritional supplements many men and women use to enhance their sexual function. Dr. Hakim presents a balanced view of the available information, including those products to avoid which may be inherently dangerous to your health, as well as those shown to be effective, as presented at recent international female sexual dysfunction meetings.

At the conclusion of this book in Part VII, with what Dr. Hakim calls the "Relationship Enhancement Program", he reemphasizes the importance of *communication* between the couple. A simple *eight-step plan* is presented in order to help the couple improve both their sexual health and intimacy on their way to an enhanced sexual relationship. Further useful information for sexually active couples, including an easy to understand overview of the often 'taboo' topic of sexually transmitted diseases, as well as a list of helpful organizations and recommended reading list, is included for the interested reader.

Because the area of sexual dysfunction has been a forbidden topic until recently, the field of Female Sexual Dysfunction is only in its genesis. *The Couple's Disease* succeeds in providing explanations and insights into many of the newer developments in female and male sexual function and dysfunction. Most importantly, the information is presented in everyday language that can be easily understood by the general reader. As the field progresses more information will become available to the reader and to the physician. I cannot emphasize enough that treatment must be initiated only under the supervision of a physician.

Dr. Hakim's introduction of this material must be applauded. It is my hope that the presentation of this comprehensive information in such a readable and instructive format will provide invaluable assistance to the many individuals and couples who suffer, often in silence and without such knowledge, from this common problem.

—*Irwin Goldstein, MD*
Boston, Massachusetts

1. Communication Interruptus

"Brad, we have to talk about it. We can't continue to put it off."

"Not now. I've got depositions all day. You know it's my biggest case since I opened my own practice."

"It's always something."

Brad did not respond. He continued to write on a legal pad, making notes from his files, which covered most of the table.

Elizabeth withdrew into herself as she smoked and drank her coffee. He hadn't wanted to talk about it last night either, nor at any other time over the past several months. Did it happen in every marriage?

At first she thought it was her fault, that she was doing something wrong. Had she been too preoccupied with her own public relations business, too tired, or treating sex as work? She'd even gone so far as to analyze her feelings for Brad. Did she still love him? Yes. Did she still find him sexually attractive? Yes, even though he'd put on about ten to fifteen pounds over the past six months.

She'd even experimented with self-arousal and masturbation to be certain that she was able to function sexually. Brad's foreplay was also very exciting and had aroused her last night as usual despite her lurking fear he wouldn't be able to perform. Unfortunately he didn't.

That was when she'd faced the fact Brad was the one with the problem. He'd become inconsistent in bed. Sometimes during sex he went flaccid; other times he ejaculated too quickly. Both instances were leaving her tense before and during sexual intercourse. And unsatisfied afterwards. Lately, he hadn't been *lasting either way beyond one or two minutes. Yes, she was tim-ing him.*

Brad put his papers in his briefcase and got up from the table. "I'm going over to the office. I'll be late. Don't wait on dinner for me."

After he left, Elizabeth lit her third cigarette of the morning. She looked at it with disgust before inhaling. Brad's lack of communication and her physical frustration had caused her to take up smoking again after she'd quit cold turkey a little over four years ago. The only person Elizabeth felt comfortable with speaking about their problem was her gynecologist, who'd rec-ommended Prozac® and that she and Brad see a sex therapist. She didn't want any "feel good" medications, and he said he'd never go to a shrink.

The house was quiet. They had no children, no time for them yet, because of their demanding careers. No pets either. She wished she could confide in a dog or cat, even an unblinking goldfish would do.

Elizabeth had postponed confiding in her best friend. She hadn't wanted to burden her with so personal a problem. Now she felt she had no choice.

She got up and went over to the phone. "Hi, mom ... "

Introduction

By Lawrence S. Hakim, MD, FACS

Life is better lived when sexual satisfaction is achieved and sustained with a loving partner. When that happens, couples experience longer, healthier relationships together, enhanced happiness, and a general sense of well being.

Divinely created or Darwinian evolved in origin, humans have had one consistent overriding *obsession*: Sex. Romantic love, on the other hand, is a relatively recent human phenomenon, supposedly popularized by medieval Arabic poetry and refined in the 12th century by the troubadours of Provence and the duchy of Aquitaine's Court of Love.

Unlike the lower animals, we are not seasonal. At all times, we think and fantasize about sex, experience it, remember it, or spend time and resources trying to prevent others from enjoying it with laws and censorship. We adorn ourselves for it, seek wealth, fame, or power for it, scheme for it, marry for it, and even ruin our lives for it. Some have murdered for it. Duels have been fought over it. That consistent, most human obsession has led to experiments, exploration, and even myths regarding sexual function and how to sustain or reclaim it.

From my experience as a physician and surgeon urologist, I now know that sexual dysfunction is in many situations a *disease:* Yes, a Couple's Disease. That opinion is also supported by *Webster's Third New International Dictionary*, which defines Disease as *"any impairment of the normal state of a living being or any of its components that modifies or interrupts the performance of vital functions."*

Although I am a male urologist by gender, women should feel secure that I understand their biological nature. The quality not the gender of a physician is what truly matters. I treat the *couple*. Gynecologists, other physicians, and sex therapists of *both genders* regularly refer their patients to me.

I treat the couple, both men and women who are having problems of sexual dysfunction. In fact, the percent of women with Female Sexual Dysfunction (FSD) whom I see individually in my practice increases each year.

I want to address another point head-on in this introduction. Unfortunately both scientists and non-scientists alike often times take absolutist positions. I'm sure you are familiar with the debates over nurture vs. nature, heredity vs. environment, creationism vs. evolution and many others. True, an extreme position may be partially correct, as a stopped clock is correct twice a day. The cautious person, however, will observe that motives of reputation and finances or the fanaticism of "the true believer" may be the real reason for an unwillingness to accept a ground somewhere between the either-or.

In the field of sexual dysfunction (SD), absolutists generally take the following positions: That it is first, foremost, and *only* caused by psychological issues or *only* by physical problems; that it can be successfully treated *only* by a sex therapist; or that *only* a female physician or sex therapist can understand a woman's body and mind. Wrong in all cases!

SD can afflict young and old alike and negatively impact a couple's quality of life. More often than not, it also can be a warning that something else may be organically awry, which, in turn does affect the human psyche.

This comprehensive book clearly addresses not only the causes of and cures for sexual dysfunction in women and men as couples and as individuals, but also its *prevention*. *The Couple's Disease* is equally as valid for sexually healthy young women and men in their 20s and 30s, as it is for couples in their 80s and 90s, and for those with either *hetero* or *same sex* preferences.

Although the focus of this book emphasizes the latest diagnoses and treatments for Female Sexual Dysfunction, as the title proclaims SD is a *couple's disease*, which is why the latest information on Male Erectile Dysfunction — its causes, cures, and possibly prevention — is also included.

The reader will receive great benefit reading about the opposite sex as well as his or her own. It will lead to better understanding of one's partner, which can be a giant step towards a more fulfilling sex life.

The purpose of *The Couple's Disease* is not to advocate unbridled sexual license. It has been written to help the individual and especially couples in love reach, improve, or continue a healthy, mutually satisfying sexual relationship *well into their "golden years"*.

Although medically sound, *The Couple's Disease* is *not* authored for physicians. SD (mostly male ED) has been covered in countless medical textbooks and journals. This book has been written for the reader who has no medical degree. For those interested in further technical information, a useful list of suggested reading appears at the end of this book.

Also, *The Couple's Disease* has *not* been written to depress the reader with statistics that can make one feel inadequate or that she or he might be missing something. Instead, I am offering the reader my *enormous resources* derived from diagnosing and successfully treating thousands of individuals and couples who have experienced Sexual Dysfunction.

STDs (sexually transmitted diseases) should be discussed because they also are a couple's problem. I have chosen to place appropriate information about these diseases, which impact both personal health and relationships, in Appendix A.

I will offer proven solutions to diverse FSD and MED problems. I will also introduce *The Plan*, which might require lifestyle changes, exercise, healthful nutrition and proven remedies. That regimen may cure early and mild FSD and MED and also help to *prevent* or slow down its progression if started early in life.

Women *are* different from men physiologically and have a far more *complex* system of sexual response. Furthermore, within our genders, each of us is special and unique; hence, *no one treatment* for FSD or MED is right for everyone.

As you read, remember these important facts:

1. You Are Not Alone. More than *half* our female and male population over forty years of age experiences some form of sexual dysfunction. Remember too, many of those under forty are similarly afflicted or will be as part of the natural aging process, illness, or injury.

2. Be Honest With Yourself. Know what is normal sexual behavior for you, regardless of what you believe may

be the standard for others. That is the only way you will learn if you have any form of SD before you discuss the matter with your physician.

3. Because SD is essentially a *couple's disease,* honest *communication* and *intimacy* between partners is the essential first step to be taken toward seeking proper help and a cure. Making love, sex, or sharing intimacy is a couple's activity. Both partners must be committed to seeking a remedy.

4. Changes in lifestyle, diet, and medications, or taking certain nutritional supplements will sustain, enhance, or restore sexual function for all except moderate or most severe cases of SD, which can be treated successfully and even *cured* with the latest medical and surgical innovations.

Ask yourself these questions before you begin reading. How and when do you know if you are not functioning normally? Is the cause of your SD psychological, physiological, or both? Remember, even women and men with a clearly organic or physical cause of their sexual dysfunction may in fact have a significant psychological or anxiety component, which can worsen the situation.

An *italicized* narrative will run throughout this book dramatizing case histories of my patients. Some are composites. Most of the dialogue is taken verbatim from conversations with my patients and letters they have written to me.

Based on my experience in treating thousands of couples who have had sexual dysfunction, I know that *every* partnership will be able to benefit from the information in *The Couple's Disease* and make their lives *better*. By following the few simple steps in my Couple's Relationship Enhancement Program, you will strengthen your communication and intimacy, improve your lifestyle, and fix any sexual problem you may have.

In short, *The Couple's Disease* will help you find the "cure" for your lost love life.

PART I

A *COUPLE'S* DISEASE

.

2. Worse than Cancer?

"Glad you could make it on such short notice, mom." Elizabeth touched wineglasses with her mother in a comfortable booth
at Brasserie La Cigale in Delray Beach.

*"It's always wonderful to receive a surprise invitation to lunch
from my baby girl,"* Mrs. Waldeck said, *"although I suspect
you've a problem you want to discuss with me."*

"How did you know? Mother's intuition?"

"That, and you've taken up smoking again."

"About a week ago."

"Everything okay with your PR firm?"

"Yes, we're doing very well."

"Then what is it ... Brad?"

"We're not ... we've been having problems in the bedroom."

*"I suppose every marriage or long-term relationship goes
through it sooner or later,"* Mrs. Waldeck said.

"Not you and dad."

*"Elizabeth, your father and I are no different from any other
couple. Our marriage might have ended because of our particular bedroom problem."*

"I didn't know. What happened? When? Why?"

"Calm yourself, darling. Everything's all right now."

"Can you tell me what happened?"

*"Yes, I think I should. And then you'll tell me what's going
on with you and Brad."*

"That's why I wanted to see you."

*"I remember when you were around twelve how shocked you
were to realize that your father and I actually made love with
each other on a regular basis."*

3

"Yes, to then I hadn't made the connection between my birth and Vicki's, and making love."

Mrs. Waldeck sipped her wine. "Our particular problem developed slowly and reached a crisis point about the time you were in grad school."

"I never suspected."

"Of course not. You were away at school, and we put on an act whenever you and your sister came home to visit. It was something only your dad and I could work out." Mrs. Waldeck paused until the food server brought their salads and left. "I have to go back in time to give you proper context. A few months after I gave birth to you, your father was diagnosed with cancer ..."

"Oh, no!"

"... and one of his testicles had to be removed."

"Poor dad. Does Vicki know?"

"No, your sister was only two and had no idea what was going on. Needless to say, we were emotionally devastated. I loved Fred so very much, as I do today, and there was the possibility he might die. Thank God, he was treated successfully and made a full recovery. Wait. I know what you're going to ask, and no, it didn't interfere with our sex life. In fact, the crisis strengthened our relationship and love for each other."

Elizabeth fussed with her salad. "Then the problem you and dad were having ... it's recent?"

"Relatively, yes. It began during your first year in grad school when you were away at the university, about the time Vicki married. We'd always had a very active sex life until things went wrong. Your father became embarrassed and frustrated when he couldn't perform consistently, and I began to blame myself as well as also being frustrated. We argued more and lost our ability to communicate, lost our intimacy too."

"Why? Was dad cheating on you?"

"Never." Mrs. Waldeck drank her wine. "You know your father has diabetes."

4

"Yes, I've seen him take his insulin."

"Diabetes can cause a man to lose his sexual function. With some, it may be a gradual decline over a period of several years. That's what happened to your dad. Then it reached the point where he couldn't achieve or maintain an erection. By then, of course, both of us were doing everything to avoid having sex. And to be honest, I was having arousal problems. Fortunately my gynecologist was familiar with that syndrome and recommended we see an expert on sexual dysfunction."

"A sex therapist?"

"No, she recommended we see Dr. Hakim."

"Is she a gynecologist?"

Mrs. Waldeck laughed and said, "Oh, no, **he** is a urologist."

"A male and a urologist? I've always gone to female doctors."

"In a crisis situation, you should seek out the best available. Dr. Hakim is one of the few experts in the United States specializing in both male **and** female sexual dysfunction. We've never had so thorough an evaluation. He also found the cause of my arousal problems. It was hormonal, not psychological. And your father liked him from the start, more so after Dr. Hakim's diagnosis and treatments restored his sexual function and the intimacy we'd known before." Mrs. Waldeck reached into her purse. "I've his card somewhere in here. Ah! Here it is. But a word of advice. Dr. Hakim prefers to see both partners."

"Brad doesn't like the idea of going to what he calls a shrink. Maybe your urologist will be less threatening. Brad's due for a physical anyway."

Mrs. Waldeck handed Elizabeth the card. "And now, will you tell me exactly what has been going on with you and Brad?"

By the time coffee arrived, Elizabeth finished describing what she'd been going through with Brad. 'So, that's where we are at this point. No sex, no communication."

"You asked for my advice. Well, here it is. Take out your cell phone now and make an appointment with Dr. Hakim for you

5

and Brad." She reached across the table and took Elizabeth's hand. "Although cancer is horrible, life-threatening, and life-taking, your father's scare brought us closer and deepened our love for each other. It may seem odd for me to say this, but in our case, sexual dysfunction was a worse disease than cancer for survivors because it drove us apart and nearly was fatal to our marriage and our relationship. As Dr. Hakim reminds us over and over, sexual dysfunction is truly a couple's disease."

ONE

Vive La Difference!

Do you look back wistfully to the time when you and your partner first became intimate and wonder how you got from there to here? A once-exciting sex life can become predictable and boring, to the point where it just feels like another chore.

If you lack interest in sex, find it difficult to get aroused, have trouble experiencing orgasms during intercourse, I must restate that *you are not alone.* Up to 50 percent of women in the United States have some form of sexual dysfunction, and almost as many men. What is more surprising, some are in their 20s and 30s, even their late teens.

We know that your sex life may not be the most comfortable topic of conversation, especially when it is not going well. The good news is that by discussing it with your partner and your doctor you will have already decided to do something about your problem.

I cannot stress enough that any form of sexual dysfunction can be a first sign of serious organic problems. Early evaluation and diagnosis of SD allows for immediate intervention, prevention, or treatment of those problems too.

That is why I want to pose a few brief questions that are designed to get you thinking about your own or your partner's sexual function and if either or both of you are experiencing mild to severe sexual dysfunction.

Women, do you have pain or discomfort during sexual intercourse? Do you experience dryness during intercourse? How would you describe your level of sexual desire? Very low, low, moderate or high? Are you satisfied with your sex life? Are you satisfied in your sexual relationship with your partner? Do you experience orgasm during intercourse and/or other forms of sexual stimulation? Have you experienced a change in your clitoral sensation? Are you able to become sexually aroused?

Men, have you noticed a change in your erections? Are they less rigid? Less spontaneous? Poorly sustained? Is your desire or libido decreased? Do you notice any penile curvature? Do you ejaculate too quickly? Are you having fewer nighttime or morning erections?

If your answers suggest any degree of a problem, you may be experiencing some form of sexual dysfunction. If so, after reading this book, you are encouraged to discuss this problem and the many available treatment options with your doctor, preferably a physician specializing in the treatment of sexual dysfunction.

Some believe that women and men are from different planets. In fact, men and women *are* different physiologically, psychologically, and emotionally. Often times they have different expectations from sex. These differences should be recognized and celebrated.

Typically, men are much more visual, women more emotional.

"Men don't want to cuddle," is a female complaint frequently heard.

Contemporary humorists have joked that some men may use intimacy to get sex, while certain women use sex to achieve intimacy. No matter what our motives might be, many individuals do not understand their partners' needs and may have false biases towards the opposite sex.

NEWS FLASH: A recent international study revealed that the major difference between the genders is that men prefer to have sex on any days starting with "T."

> *Tuesday*
> *Thursday*
> *Thanksgiving*
> *Today*
> *Tomorrow*
> *Thaturday*
> *Thunday.*

And to refute a cliché that always associates women and lack of sex with headaches, according to various studies, at least half a million American men and women, most otherwise healthy, experience coital (sex) headaches, which can occur at or near orgasm. *Men are the primary sufferers from these headaches, up to 80 percent of reported cases.*

These headaches appear at the base of the skull and create intense pain that can last up to fifteen minutes. They can occur during sexual intercourse or masturbation. The reasons why fewer females experience these headaches are not agreed upon, although some experts theorize that endorphin release with vaginal stimulation may block pain, as if preparing a woman for childbirth.

9

This syndrome is sometimes temporary but curable if it persists. If you or your partner suffer from frequent coital headaches, evaluation by a qualified physician would be a prudent first step to take. Treatments can include biofeedback, healthier diet combined with cardiovascular exercise and weight loss. Also, certain preventive medications are available that can be taken before sexual activity.

TWO

You Are Not Alone

If you, as either a woman or a man, have any form of Sexual Dysfunction, remember this: You are not alone. In truth, you are statistically in the majority once you pass the age of forty. *For those under that age who are afflicted with problems of SD, the statistics from validated studies will emphasize the truth that you also are not alone.*

Some may disagree that SD is a disease. However, statistics will bear out that SD is an epidemic of vast proportions. Sexual Dysfunction affects more than 50-million women and men in the United States. If it were a virus or bacteria, our government would call SD a pandemic.

Currently, less than one-third of men with Erectile Dysfunction seek help.

Currently, only 5 percent to 10 percent of women with FSD seek help.

If you prefer, think of SD as a non-threatening part of the aging process. You may be doing things less efficiently, might be less strong, but you can still perform the same activities. By the end of this book, you will learn how to slow, if not delay, the aging process within the realm of sexual function and, perhaps, the entire aging process.

You can also compare SD to a physical injury, from minor to serious. If you had a tennis partnership, and your teammate suffered a sprain, you know that he or she would not be performing up to par, but would be 100 percent in a very short time. If it were a broken leg or arm, you would not demand your partner get on the court right away.

Of course sport injuries and medical ailments are obvious and easily spoken of. Traditionally, most women and men have been reluctant to speak openly to their partners about their sexual dysfunction. Unfortunately, most physicians also fail to ask their patients, during the course of evaluation and treatments for other ailments, if they are satisfied with their sexual function.

Normal sexual function is an important part of the **essential intimacy** between partners *(the couple)*. Sexual dysfunction obviously leads to loss of self-esteem, depression, and alienation between partners.

And no matter how mild or severe the condition, sexual dysfunction is curable.

First, understand what is normal for you and *only you* in matters of your libido and sex drive.

Next, communicate, communicate, communicate with your mate or lover. Sexual dysfunction, I repeat, is a couple's problem.

Of course, most women and men have difficulty discussing their sexual function, since the subject is so personal. Who among us has not been educated from first memories that our genitalia will always be our "private parts"? Interestingly, this was also the title of Howard Stern's wildly popular book and movie.

True intimacy and *understanding* of each other's needs, desires, and yes, even fantasies, are also essential to a successful relationship. Decreased sexual activity with your partner can lead to less intimacy and ultimately the breakup of relationships in our contemporary era in which there is literally a smorgasbord of other partners and options.

If over time you become used to less or no sex, then the couple is less likely to seek treatment because the interest may no longer exist. I believe that the couple must discuss their specific issues of SD and seek help as soon as it becomes a problem, so that their relationship can not only be salvaged but also their intimacy improved. Unfortunately, delayed treatment may come too late to restore intimacy or save the relationship.

Sexual dysfunction is usually a continuum ranging from mild to severe. Early warning signs can be missed. If detected and treated early, reversal and even elimination of SD can improve your quality of life and prevent more invasive treatments.

Remember, sexual dysfunction can be an expected outcome of various procedures and other factors. For example, menopause, hysterectomy and pelvic surgery in women and surgical removal of the prostate gland in men can cause SD.

Understanding that SD may occur from those events, alerted women and men should immediately seek treatment to restore normal sexual function. If the patient sees SD as an *outcome* not a *complication*, then the process of *rehabilitation* or restoring normal function can begin, rather than waiting and risking the end of a relationship without sex and intimacy.

Prevention, rejuvenation, and restoration with the goal of a return to normal sexual function are part of the same model as restoring normal physical and mental health after an illness. Never forget that good sexual health, a sense of well-being, and a positive self-image are often indispensable parts of a complete and happy person.

If you and your partner can achieve true intimacy, you will have accomplished the first goal of this book. I truly believe that better communication and better sex will improve all aspects of your relationship as a couple.

Another objective of this book is to help the reader identify the early warning signs of SD and possibly prevent sexual dysfunction from occurring or at least to delay its onset, which is why I feel that even young men and women may benefit from reading this book. If SD does begin to appear, I will explain why you should seek treatment early and all the current options that are available, as well as some of the latest breakthroughs.

The worst-case scenario is to wait until the male is completely impotent or the woman loses total interest in sex with her partner, cannot become aroused to orgasm or finds the pain during intercourse unbearable.

Problems with SD can end the thrill that brought the couple together. Stating the obvious, lack of sex and communication with your partner often leads to affairs, cheating, and ultimately breaking up or divorce.

I have seen time and time again in my practice that even young women and men in their 20s and 30s may notice changes in their sexual function. One partner or the other may begin to experience SD or lack of desire for sex based on many factors. They may be symptoms of either potentially serious organic problems such as diabetes and vascular diseases, especially those caused by cigarette smoking, atherosclerosis (blocked arteries) and high cholesterol. Other factors include lifestyle problems caused by stress, childbirth, trauma to the genitalia (such as that caused by bicycle riding to be discussed in subsequent chapters) overuse of alcohol, misuse of illegal drugs, side-effects of medications, or even the wrong herbals. Commonly, females with a history of childhood sexual abuse or even molestation can have marked serious problems with their sexual desire and arousal.

It is not all that unusual for men in their 30s and 40s to notice changes in morning and nighttime erections, erection sustainability, or even arousal.

As I previously stated, SD is often a continuum of disease. In most cases, *early* manifestations of SD in women and men can easily be treated and possibly reversed with lifestyle changes, use of herbal or hormonal supplements, prescription medications such as Viagra®(sildenafil citrate from Pfizer), and other successfully tested pharmaceuticals. Others are still under investigation and may be approved for consumer use within the next few years.

To reinforce what I have said, that you are not alone, let's look at some of the various studies and statistics relating to sexual dysfunction.

3. Dr. Hakim's Waiting Room

Elizabeth was surprised at the number of women and men in Dr. Hakim's waiting room. Including herself, there were fifteen, some obviously couples. She guessed the age range ran from her 28 years to a couple in their late 70s or early 80s. One or two men seemed to be in their 20s or early 30s, around Brad's age. That ought to give him some comfort.

Elizabeth had at last convinced her husband that they were having a serious problem. One of her virtues, which some people called a fault, was her frankness and honesty. Brad had not been comfortable when she suggested they see Dr. Hakim, whom her mother had recommended. It had taken plenty of coaxing … nagging, he called it … until he finally agreed to rearrange his schedule and meet her here today.

Elizabeth sat next to a lean, wiry athletic looking woman she guessed to be in her early to mid-thirties. Close to my age, she thought, and then checked her watch. Two-thirty. She was an hour early. Brad often teased her about being a "Prussian Virgo". No argument there. Not only was she fussy and precise, she had a fetish about never being late for an appointment and often arrived up to an hour early.

Elizabeth looked at her watch again and sighed. Would Brad really show up?

THREE

Believe Them: Validated Studies That Prove You Are Not Alone

With the introduction of Viagra, increased media attention has pushed "Female Sexual Dysfunction" into the spotlight. More and more, women are beginning to understand that their sexual problems may be *organic* in nature and that treatment is available.

As you read, however, remember that *you* are *you*, a *unique* human being, and that each treatment for SD is individualized. So, *do not* measure yourself against statistical norms. No single treatment is right for every one.

Physicians Lambert and Rosen in a recent study published in the Journal of the American Medical Association (JAMA) and others of equal repute have shown that SD is more prevalent in women (43 percent) than in men (31 percent). Those same studies reveal that SD affects young and old, and often is symptomatic of other, even life-threatening, problems such as diabetes or cardiovascular disease.

In another study by Dr. Laumann, the conclusion was that "aging" as a cause of SD is not as significant a factor in women as with men, especially from ages 18-59. As compared to men, who generally have decreased erectile function with aging, women have no such equivalent relationship. Virtually the same percent of FSD occurs in women in their 20s, 30s, 40s, and 50s.

Although certain medical conditions may affect the sexual function of older, post-menopausal women, the fact is that FSD is also prevalent in younger women. Based on population surveys, Laumann's study and others suggest that at least 30 million women in the USA might have some form of FSD.

Various demographic studies as well as a recent study of 200 women, mean age 42 years, at a Boston sexual health clinic revealed various high risk factors for FSD that included the usual suspects: High cholesterol, smoking, depression, certain anti-depressant medications, birth control pills, hysterectomies, post-menopausal hormonal imbalance, and diabetes.

Dr. Nancy E. Avis of Wake-Forest Medical School analyzed another study from Massachusetts of approximately 200 menopausal women who had a current sexual partner. She concluded that they were generally *satisfied* with their sexual relationships and had sex on the average *a little over once a week.* Compare *that* with what you are told by the popular media.

Regarding men, according to the 1994 Massachusetts Male Aging Study, the incidence of erectile dysfunction amongst men over 40 is 52 percent. After 70, it can be as high as 85 percent.

Sexual dysfunction is not only a problem for older couples, as you will learn in greater detail throughout this book. A greater number of younger women than one might expect also suffer from FSD.

Here are the results of a Female Sexual Dysfunction Study in which I recently co-investigated. 150 women were evaluated with ages ranging from 25 to 82. Of note, 56 percent of the women had FSD, which caused personal distress, a decrease in sexual desire and activity, decreased vaginal lubrication and difficulty achieving orgasm. 17 percent had mild FSD, 20 percent had moderate FSD and 19 percent had severe FSD.

The most common risk factors were age over 50, previous hysterectomy, cigarette smoking, high cholesterol levels and high blood pressure. In fact, for a significant number of women with FSD our study identified for the first time that they had some specific lipid or blood fat abnormality (hypercholesterolemia), mainly due to high cholesterol.

In another study in which I co-investigated, we discovered that 53 percent of women who have partners with Erectile Dysfunction also have some form of FSD themselves.

19

FOUR

Should We Believe
Everything We Are Told?

In this era of sexually explicit talk shows and mega-exposure to every aspect of sexuality in all media, such as HBO's hit shows *Real Sex* and *Sex in the City*, a common sense question arises: What is "normal" sexual function?

A recent survey took place on the *Redbook* and *Esquire* web sites conducted by Fairfield Research, Inc., on behalf of *Redbook Magazine*. The purpose was to document sexual attitudes and behavior of men and women. The survey received 10,415 individually completed questionnaires from 7,757 women and 2,658 men.

Some of the more interesting findings are described below. Only 34 percent of women stated that they always reach orgasm during sex, compared to 82 percent of men. 79 percent of women stated they enjoyed sex, versus 92 percent of men. Both men and women (70 percent) agreed that sex is better when they are in a committed relationship. Interestingly, only 20 percent of women and 17 percent of men were "extremely happy" with their current sexual activity. Of interest, the majority of women (59 percent) and men (85 percent) reported they would rather have sex than shop, sleep, eat or watch television. Bad news for ratings and advertisers?

Of interest, 23 percent of women and 29 percent of men admitted that they cheated on their partners; of those, 31 percent of each sex admitted to having had an affair with a married man or woman. Missing from those figures are the causes. Could a partner's SD, lack of intimacy, or poor communication be the reason?

Believe or disbelieve, as you might political polls, the following have appeared recently in various publications and news releases:

- 7 to 10 percent of men in their 30s have trouble sustaining an erection. In those situations, the doctors concluded, most causes are *psychological.*

- 30 percent of men ages 25 to 40 say they experience premature ejaculation.

- About 14 percent of women between 20 and 39 admit their major sexual problem is that they climax *too early.*

Finally, a recent study reported by the NIH (National Institutes of Health) compared sexual activity among 3,000 African American, Asian, Caucasian, Chinese, and Japanese women across the United States.

Seventy-eight percent of women in this study reported that they had engaged in partnered sex during the past 6 months, and 32 percent said sex was quite or extremely important.

Reasons for no sexual activity included lack of a partner, fatigue, and lack of interest.

When compared with Caucasians, Japanese and Chinese women were less likely to report sex as very important; African American women were more likely to report sex as important.

Not included in the above surveys are those under the age of 18. A study published a few years ago in JAMA found that more than 16 percent of 12 and 13 year olds had already experienced sexual intercourse. At the rate our popular culture, especially the visual media, promote promiscuity, one can expect those numbers to increase. Unfortunately, they most likely lead to more teenage pregnancies, illegitimate births, and sexually transmitted diseases or STDs (see Appendix A).

Other studies abound in the print media as well as quotes by MDs, Ph.Ds, and other "sexperts". During the so-called quiet or conforming 1950s, an event occurred that forever changed the dialogue about sex in the United States — the publication of Hugh Hefner's *PLAYBOY*. After that, the gates to sexual information opened wider and wider.

Radio, popular magazines, cable and network TV have also made especially valuable contributions to giving the general public a broader and more complete understanding of our sexuality. We should give credit to publishers, talk show pioneers and current hosts for using their power to bring these incredibly personal issues out into the open. They include: Oprah, Larry King, Dr. Ruth Westheimer, Dr. Laura Schlessinger, Bob Guccione, Bill Maher, Jon Stewart, Jay Leno and David Letterman, Phil Donohue, Jerry Springer and so many others.

Of special note, Howard Stern, as well as Adam and Dr. Drew of Loveline, deserve an incredible amount of credit (albeit controversial to some viewers). They also have brought honest discussion out into the open, helped to show that sex isn't "dirty", and shed a brighter light on our sexuality, especially for young people and "late night" viewers.

By pushing the envelope of the conversation, these pioneers make it easier for all of us to realize that when it comes to sexual problems, we are not alone, its OK to talk about sex, and excellent treatments are out there for the asking.

FIVE

What About The Rest Of The World?

What we are discussing refers *not only* to the population of the United States. You have been told that you are not alone. Well, our country also is not alone! My personal experiences lecturing and performing surgical impotence procedures in countries as diverse as South Korea, Spain, Australia, Turkey, and Brazil along with research and studies from various parts of the world will be cited throughout this book to illustrate that sexual dysfunction is a global disease of epidemic proportions.

What follows are assorted facts and statistics from overseas. They are but a few among many. Some may be the result of sound research; others reflect random statistics and interviews.

DATE LINE: JAPAN!

An estimated 9.8-million Japanese men suffer from erectile dysfunction.

TOKYO (Reuters) — A soft drink containing an ingredient of the impotence drug Viagra has been banned by Japanese officials. They acted after advertisements for the drink, touted as the solution to "your nighttime problems," appeared in a men's magazine and on the Internet.

Some 47,000 bottles of the non-prescription drink were imported from China ... all but 4,000 sold.

Each bottle of the drink contained 64.3 mg of sildenafil, the active ingredient in Viagra, far more than the 25 or 50 mg in one tablet sold in Japan. Each 20-millimeter bottle was priced at 3,000 yen ($25.70), compared with 1,000 to 1,300 yen per tablet for Viagra.

An official said the drug contravened Japanese drug laws.

DATELINE: ARGENTINA!

A recent study from Argentina presented at an International FSD Society meeting revealed that 63 percent of women aged 18-75 had some difficulties with sexual desire, 30 percent had sexual arousal problems, 20 percent had difficulties achieving orgasm, and 13 percent had vaginal pain.

Overall, one-third of these women reported dissatisfaction with their sex life, especially amongst those over 40 years of age. Various risk factors proved significant in this study, including hypertension (**hyper** being greater than normal), hypercholesterolemia, and results of having had gynecological surgery.

DATELINE: SCOTLAND!

Edinburgh Psychologist David Weeks and Science writer Jamie James, authors of the book, *Secrets of the*

Superyoung, interviewed 95 elderly people in Scotland who looked young for their ages. They were surprised to learn that sex was a major factor causing their subjects' youthful appearance. In fact, they claimed that *vigorous regular sex* could make one look seven years younger. Why? Energetic lovemaking can reduce fatty tissue and release endorphins from the brain, which are natural painkillers and reduce anxiety.

DATELINE: THE WORLD!

According to a global survey of 18,000 male "consumers" aged 16 to 25 by SSL International, British manufacturer of *Durex®* condoms, Americans have sex most often. But the French boast of having the most sexual partners.

How many times a year is the survey speaking of? Americans, 132; Russians, 122; French 121; and the Greeks 115. Americans were quickest to lose their virginity, while older teens and young adults in Japan engaged in sexual activity the least.

Most Americans said they learned about sex from their fathers, while the Dutch replied it was from their mothers. Italians claimed they learned about sex from their brothers and sisters, while the French gave credit to their bed partners.

The following claimed these average totals for sexual partners in a given year: French, 16.7, Greeks, 15, Brazilians 12.5, and Americans at 11.8. Indians were the most faithful to their partners, with 82 percent claiming they had sex with only one person.

Americans were the earliest to have sex at 16.4 years, closely followed by Brazilians at 16.5 and the French at 16.8.

The survey revealed that 61 percent of those ages 16-20, and 52 percent of those ages 21-24 preferred condoms for contraception. 13 percent said they used no form of contraception, while 8 percent stated they used natural methods.

American males also lead the "sexual Olympics" according to *The Social Organization of Sexuality* by Laumann, Gagnon, Michael, and Michaels, University of Chicago Press, 1994. American men have sex 6 times a month, or 72 times a year. Young Japanese made love the least at 37 times a year, Malaysians 62 times, the Chinese 69 times.

4. Dr. Hakim's Waiting Room

Elizabeth made eye contact with the young woman. "My husband is meeting me here. Do you know if the doctor prefers to see us as a couple or individually?"

"From what I've seen, it depends on their comfort level. By the way I'm Lauren."

"Elizabeth."

"If I may ask, who has the problem?"

"I think it's him. Why are you here?"

"I lost the ability to have orgasms with my husband. Oh, I could reach it using Viagra and a vibrator, but that took a lot of effort."

Lauren's frankness shocked Elizabeth, who guessed the young woman needed someone to talk to. "How did your husband react to that?"

"At first, he thought I was avoiding sex because I no longer cared for him. It affected his performance too. Dr. Hakim is right when he refers to sexual dysfunction as a couple's disease. We're okay now since he knows the reason why. He was ... still is ... a supportive, loving partner. Dr. Hakim said that what made it easy for him to treat me is that Jack and I have an open relationship. My husband has normal sexual function, is sexually sophisticated, and knows how to stimulate me."

Elizabeth wished she could say that about Brad.

SIX

Communicate, Communicate, Communicate!

The worst thing women and men can do regarding their sexual function is to "measure" themselves against the presumed libido and performances of others. Also, the reader must forget many socially accepted myths about Sexual Dysfunction:

That it is just "in your mind."

That it is an inevitable consequence of aging.

True, **psychological** and/or **societal** factors are involved in ALL cases, but they more likely will signal an underlying physical cause. To the contrary, sexual dysfunction is often due to physical or organic causes. SD can occur at any age, young or old.

Normal according to what you may read or hear is not necessarily *normal.*

Specific couple's issues can cause mild to severe sexual dysfunction. They can include poor or no communication, relationship difficulties, selfish love, lack of attraction and poor chemistry, poor technique, power issues, infidelity, illness, poor hygiene, and sexual abuse both emotional and physical. Consider how the following can impact a couple's sexual relationship:

A permissive society offers more opportunities to stray.

Some may fear that sex toys might be preferred to a partner.

Understand how a changing global economy affects the traditional family and its values. In fact, a recent study suggested that less than 50 percent of families in the U.S. are "traditional", with a mother, father, and kids. And even amongst those families, more women are in the workplace, which adds to their daily stressors, aside from taking care of children and self, as well as interacting with extended family (siblings, parents, and in-laws). All that leaves little time for intimacy with her spouse.

> **NEWS FLASH:** *In England, the Chartered Institute of Personnel and Development polled 486 Britons who work 48 hours per week. More than a third of those surveyed admitted that work-related tiredness caused their sex lives to suffer and 14 percent reported loss of, or reduced desire. 42 percent cited their partner's long hours on the job caused arguments at home, which most certainly does not contribute to a healthy sex life.*
>
> *The survey also found that these workaholics tended to be male, middle-aged, and married. 54 percent of their partners said that their sex lives suffered because of the long hours, and 43 percent were resentful at having to deal with most of the domestic burden.*

In addition, sensual overload from an overabundance of Internet, online and VCR pornography can lead to jaded tastes and more extreme experiments in sex to achieve enhanced performance and satisfaction, in which a partner may not wish to participate.

The good news is that Sexual Dysfunction can always be treated to a couple's satisfaction. In some cases it may also be reversed and even prevented.

Early expert evaluation, counseling, and treatment (if necessary) can assure a successful outcome.

◆ ◆ ◆

First and foremost, true lovers must communicate positively. You should avoid playing the "Blame Game" when either you or your partner fails to function sexually. Each partner should feel free to express concerns and fears and openly discuss the condition of FSD and/or ED as a first step to a cure.

For younger couples, the problem may be temporary, caused by sexual immaturity, stress, insufficient sleep, lack of privacy because children intrude, and external societal pressures.

You should also question yourself. What is it you really want? For what purpose do you want to improve your libido/sex life? Are you seeking self or mutual gratification, love or a one-night stand?

Physical, not necessarily "compatibility" issues, can also cause your partner's SD. Does the male ejaculate too soon and leave his partner unsatisfied? Does the female suffer real clitoral or vaginal pain, or is unable to reach orgasm? And in turn, does she create excuses not to engage in sexual intercourse with her partner? Remember too, that job stress, home stress, and the responsibilities of raising children affect both partners' commitment to energized sexual interaction.

Also one might want to please the other by having sex when not in the mood, which turns a potentially wonderful experience into work, a job.

Sex can also become very hard *work* during times of infertility. Young couples may try *too* hard to make a baby, which creates stress and worry instead of pleasure and intimacy.

Other causes of problems amongst couples can be a partner's denial of SD, and lack of communication regarding fantasies, poor technique, and true desires.

Why not talk openly about your sexual fantasies before sex in a non-threatening fashion. Make your partner aware of your desires: Watching her/him undress, dancing erotically, wearing suggestive garments, role-playing.

Regardless, again the couple is urged to communicate. Otherwise, your satisfaction will not be achieved, one or both may stray, and SD often follows. If this is difficult, seek help and guidance in building communication skills. For many couples, relationship counseling can help them learn those necessary skills.

To state the obvious: Sexual dysfunction affects self-esteem, self-confidence, and quality of life for both partners. Because SD is a couple's disease, your partner should be involved in its treatment and management whenever possible.

Remember too, no single treatment is right for everybody. An individualized multi-disciplinary approach is recommended, one that includes your Primary Care Physician, your Gynecologist or Urologist specializing in SD, a licensed *credible* Sex Therapist if necessary, and of most importance, your partner.

Think about how complex and unprotected our bodies are. We humans are truly "naked apes" with no thick skins, fur, or shells to protect us, and so many injuries and diseases can cause SD. That any of us can function normally is truly amazing.

Take comfort in remembering this:

All conditions of sexual dysfunction are treatable. However, it is up to you and hopefully your partner to take the first step and seek help.

SEVEN

Sex, Religion, And Myths

From early childhood, we are often given misinformation by commission and omission about sexual function and dysfunction. As we mature, that misinformation is further compounded by myths, media sensationalism, and religious teachings, or, to be generous, errors of religious dogma. Medical science is also deserving of its share of blame. Not one of us really wishes to be treated by 19th and early 20th century standards.

RELIGION:

Laws prohibiting certain sexual acts indicate a human tendency towards that behavior, which tribes and governments over several millennia have attempted to eliminate.

Sex, lust, and all the crimes and transgressions that accompany carnal desire for another person are all too evident throughout the Bible. Throughout the Old Testament, the Israelites waged war against those who worshipped "false gods" such as Baal and Ishtar with human sacrifice, ritual intercourse, fertility rites, and worse abominations in their eyes. Later, Christians also waged similar wars against pagan deities and the sexual practices of their followers.

One might take a cynical point of view and conclude that if the Judeo-Christian male could not control himself, it was best to control the female sex.

Is there any woman who has not heard her menstrual period referred to as "The Curse" as punishment of her entire sex in reference to Eve's seduction of Adam into Original Sin and causing the Fall of Man? Over the previous millennia, mothers generally did not prepare their daughters for the onset of their menstrual cycle; and even if some did, when a girl experienced her first period, religious cultural customs or religious dogma dictated that she was "unclean" or had sinned.

Religions have also condemned masturbation, the "secret vice" or "self abuse," as evil. The Judeo-Christian popular legacy is that sex or lovemaking is to be reserved for procreation only. Anything else is a sin against God.

In all dictionaries onanism/onanist are the terms for masturbation and masturbator. But they are not the first definition. *Coitus interruptus* is. As one might expect, something got lost in the translation.

Judah was the son of Jacob/Israel, grandson of Isaac, and great-grandson of Abraham. As the story goes in Genesis 38:7-11, Onan was obviously guilty of *coitus interruptus*, not the "solitary vice". But "wasted seed" is wasted seed and still a sin against God.

Consider this: A man may be "bewitched" by a woman, but when have you heard or read that a woman was "warlocked" by a man? Because of the aforementioned religious oppression of women, a man's lust was always transferred to the woman as if it were her fault that he

35

desired her. Who gets to wear the Scarlet Letter? Not the male.

MEDICINE AND SCIENCE:

The medical profession must also share some blame for negative myths about female sexuality. Over the centuries, especially during the previous three hundred years, doctors have treated normal sexual desire in women and even men as pathological.

As an example, in 1710 an anonymous quack published: *Onania, or the Heinous Sin of Self-Pollution, and all its frightful Consequences in both Sexes, Considered.* It became an international best seller. From that date, masturbation was no longer considered only a sin. It was now harmful to one's health and socially "filthy" as well. Religion now had an ally in Science.

Onania's widespread influence upon the medical and religious establishment led to parental hysteria throughout Europe regarding masturbation. Throughout the 19th and early 20th centuries, physicians warned that masturbation would lead to physical disabilities, *impotence*, sterility, ill health, insanity, and death.

The remedies included everything from beatings to torturous physical restraints for boys and girls, and even clitoridectomies (surgical removal of the clitoris). Documented horror stories describe how boys were severely mistreated with devices no less monstrous than chastity belts, not because they masturbated, but because they had simply experienced unintended ejaculations while in a dream state.

Although masturbation was a sin, physicians treated women afflicted with "hysteria" by masturbating their patients to orgasm in order to calm them, which is why some believe the vibrator was invented in the 19th century supposedly as a medical device.

We can call it Victorianism, Puritanism, prudery, or whatever. Regardless, the effects of those beliefs and values continue to *oppress us.*

NYMPHS AND VAMPIRES:

The concept of Nymphomania is a relatively recent phenomenon. Again, during the 19th century, any woman who displayed what men considered an abnormally voracious sexual appetite was viewed as ill, a nymphomaniac. Men had such great fear of sexually aggressive women that another term was coined, *vagina dentes*, the vagina with teeth, highlighting their fear of castration.

Today, that condemnatory word, nymphomania, is still widely used. Some mental health specialists continue to believe that such women are infantile, unable to reach orgasm, or are frigid. Anecdotally, many contemporary women have admitted that after divorce they were voraciously sexual for periods of many months, "in my wild phase" as these patients have said in so many words.

The male equivalent of nymphomania has been known as the Don Juan or Casanova complex. But is any male ever unflattered to be called a Casanova or Don Juan?

A more disparaging word, however, has been used to describe the over-sexed male with uncontrollable urges: Satyriasis. Nymph and Satyr! Sex as a pagan activity.

Early psychoanalysts used to say that a woman afflicted with nymphomania would end up in the madhouse; a man afflicted with satyriasis would end up in jail.

Currently, both men and women with self-destructive sexual appetites or those beyond any rational norm may be referred to as Sex Addicts, for which there is a 12-step program.

Another 19th century negative stereotype of women is the Vampire. True, Dracula was male, but the major Symbolist painters and writers frequently portrayed women as vampires, seldom men. An influential male artist might also reveal his own basic weakness, consciously or not, when he referred to an object of his slavish desire as *la femme fatale* or *la belle dame sans merci* — the fatal woman or the beautiful lady without pity.

During the early years of cinema, the female vampire became the Vamp, the courtesan who drained men not of their blood but their wealth, as *les grandes horizontales* did in 19th century France. Then she discarded them when they had nothing else to give. From Vamp, she evolved to Gold Digger and currently is referred to as being High Maintenance. The male equivalent is gigolo.

◆ ◆ ◆

If we are honest with ourselves, we will remember during our school years how we accepted as truth rumors, gossip, and misinformation about sex spread by friends and classmates. Today, the media has replaced the locker room. How many times is normal? What is the best technique for your partner to please you? How can you best please your partner? How can you best please yourself?

As mentioned earlier, women and men may be convinced something is either wrong with themselves or their partner when measured against a non-controlled media poll. Articles and books based on one person's experiences may not inspire but actually cause false expectations or discontent in the reader when none is warranted.

Based on my experience treating women and couples, I must explode another myth. Aging need not negatively impact the possibilities of a fulfilling sex life with your partner, even though you might be in your 70s, 80s, and 90s.

SEX AND AGING
20-30: Try Daily
31-40: Try Weekly
41-50: Try Weakly
51-60: Try Oysters
61-70: Try Anything
Over 70: Try to Remember

Amusing, but again rest assured that this need not happen to you.

PART II

FEMALE SEXUAL RESPONSE

5. Outside the Clinic

Lauren shook her head when Elizabeth lit a cigarette outside the clinic where Dr. Hakim had his office. "You know, I don't approve."

"Neither do I, but thanks for keeping me company. I'm so nervous. A few puffs ... then we can go back up."

"What are you specifically nervous about?"

Elizabeth didn't want to describe her sex life with Brad the way Lauren had spoken about hers. "Worry about the unknown, I guess."

"Unknown is right. Before I met Dr. Hakim, I thought I knew everything about my own body. Was I ever wrong!"

"What do you mean?"

"Like the size of my clitoris."

"Say what?"

"Bet you don't know the size of yours."

"Sure, I do. It's about the size of my thumbnail ... like most women, I assume ... maybe a bit larger when I'm aroused."

Lauren smiled and said, "Oh, Elizabeth, that's only the tip of the volcano."

EIGHT

Understanding Female Anatomy

Although the next three parts of the book focus primarily on the female sexual response and FSD, men should read Parts II, III and IV so they may better understand their female partner, which hopefully will lead to better intimacy and communication.

During the first four weeks in the mother's womb, an embryo's genitals are not sexually defined. Soon after that, genitals begin to develop as either female or male.

All in all, women have at least 12 sexual organs from the mons pubis to the anus. These include the clitoris, glans, shaft, urethra, and G-spot.

The outer female genitalia are known as the **vulva**. Going from "north" to "south", the vulva begins with the **mons pubis**, a fatty tissue that covers the pubic bone and is covered by skin and hair. Directly below the mons pubis are the **clitoral hood, clitoris, urethral opening**, and **vaginal entrance**. The **labia majora** (outer "lips") and **labia minora** (inner "lips") are "east" and "west" of the entrance to the vagina. The **perineum** lies in the "south," and the **anus** in the "deep south."

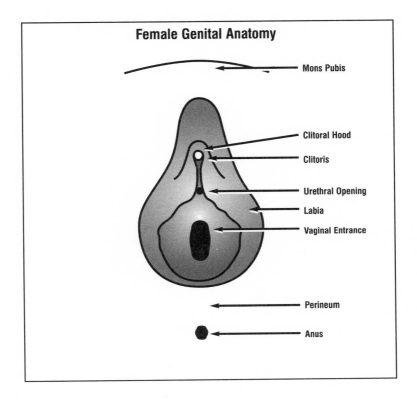

Female Genital Anatomy

Mons Pubis

Clitoral Hood

Clitoris

Urethral Opening

Labia

Vaginal Entrance

Perineum

Anus

Published studies of women and men as well as anecdotal questioning in social situations reveal that very few of them know exactly where the clitoris is located or even its size. If you feel comfortable enough with your friends, you might ask them if they know the size of the clitoris. Most people will assume that the clitoris is anywhere from a quarter inch, to 2 or more inches. In reality, the clitoris is approximately 11 centimeters or about 4 inches in length. Only its tip is initially exposed before arousal.

The clitoris is made of the *same* highly sensitive erectile tissue as the penis, a mini-penis if you will. During sexual excitement, vascular engorgement of the clitoris (its arteries filling with blood) is similar to engorgement of the male's penis.

In addition during sexual arousal, the surrounding spongy tissue of the urethra and the vagina expand and the cervix and uterus lift, which straightens and opens the vagina. Female orgasm and, yes, often ejaculation occur through stimulation of the clitoris, urethra, and surrounding tissues.

As in men, vasodilation and erection of the female clitoris is the basis of arousal, and vaginal lubrication is due to increased blood flow, in some ways analogous to penile erection in the male. The glans clitoris extends out from its 'hood' during arousal and sexual activity and engorges with enhanced sensitivity. The clitoris changes in shape during intercourse, allowing for enhanced friction and contact during the sexual act.

The clitoris has more nerves than any other organ in the female body, with all varieties of sensory receptors, all of which depend upon androgens in order to function. Therefore, without androgens, these organs become insensate (lose the ability to "feel").

Much more will be said about the importance of androgens in a woman's sexual function throughout this book. An increased understanding of the physiology of clitoral erection has led to increased options for the treatment of FSD.

The vagina contains substantial smooth-muscle which must be "relaxed" in order to fill with blood (engorgement) during the female sexual response. Studies have shown that androgens and chemicals such as alpha-blockers can act upon it. During arousal, the vagina both lengthens and widens about two inches, and swelling of the labia occurs (like "bumpers"), which makes it easier for the penis to enter the vagina.

46

A number of neurotransmitters or chemicals can increase vaginal blood flow and lubrication. Complex interactions amongst the different neurotransmitters definitely play an important role in the female sexual response. More intensive investigations are underway to give us a better understanding of their function.

The brain controls the female sexual response. Men may need only to have an erection to feel sexually adequate. In women, however, performance issues and feelings of arousal are predominantly due to the processing of stimuli at the brain level — a sort of "feedback" from the blood flow and arousal. For men increased blood flow leads to penile hardness. In women, increased blood flow leads to increased sensation. Thus, enhanced sensation is paramount to this entire process of female sexual response.

Regarding the nerve supply and sexual enervation, all the nerves in the female genitalia pass through a specific area known as Alcock's Canal, which is located anatomically in the perineum. Therefore, an injury to women in this area, as a result of bicycle riding or other blunt perineal trauma can cause diminished sensation and changes in orgasm ability.

Social issues play a role in affecting the brain and may be somewhat prohibitive when it comes to female sexual response. This reinforces how important psychological considerations are when we assess the female sexual response.

Although sildenafil (Viagra) alone may restore normal erections for men who have performance anxiety and other psychological problems, such treatment is not all that straightforward when dealing with the *more complex* female sexual response. For women experiencing FSD, pyschosexual intervention must often be combined with drug therapy to successfully restore their sexual health.

NINE

Characteristics Of The Female Sexual Response

Pioneering research by Dr. Kinsey in the 1940s and 50s and Dr. Masters and Johnson in the 1960s provided insights into the range of normal sexual function and the physiological process underlying sexual stimulation. The media, both TV and written, have popularized these studies. Unfortunately, they also created false standards of "normality".

For example, some popular periodicals and TV shows have so rigorously promoted multiple female orgasm as essential to fulfillment that they have tended to cause women to feel inadequate if they do not experience them. So once again the question comes to mind: What is normal?

Many studies of sexual function used by the media are generally fraught with various problems such as small sample numbers and are often limited to specific populations. Once again, women should know that validated studies conclude as many as 50 percent of people will experience some degree of SD during their lifetimes. Predictors include age and partner status, because many of those with complaints of SD tend to be older women without partners.

Masters (who passed away as this book was written) and Johnson's groundbreaking book on sexual response described how women and men responded to sexual stimulation. At that time they described sexual response in four stages or cycles: Excitement, Plateau, Orgasm and Resolution.

Later, Dr. Helen Singer Kaplan modified the model of the sexual cycle to include Desire, Arousal, and Orgasm. Kaplan felt that some people either do not have much sexual desire or do not become sexually aroused. That is why she considered Desire to be the first stage of sexual response.

After Dr. Kaplan, the American Psychiatric Association defined sexual response in four related stages: Desire or Libido; Arousal or Excitement; Orgasm or Climax; and a Refractory Period or Resolution. Women in the field of treating FSD were especially dissatisfied with the DSM-IV definitions, as they were known, which did not adequately differentiate between the genders.

In March 2000, the International Female Sexual Dysfunction panel met to determine and define exactly what FSD is. The DSM-IV had previously stated a woman could be determined to have FSD if her *partner* complained she didn't get aroused or become orgasmic enough. This was not acceptable to the panel.

The panel developed a new Female Sexual Disorders Classification, which then appeared in the *Journal of Urology*: Female Sexual Desire Disorders; Hypoactive Sexual Disorder (**hypo** being below normal); Sexual Aversion

Disorder; Sexual Arousal Disorder; Orgasmic Disorder; and Sexual Pain Disorders (Dyspareunia, Vaginismus, and non-coital pain disorder). Furthermore:

1. Symptoms must be persistent over issues of desire, arousal, and/or ability to reach orgasm under normal sexual activity for at least 3 months duration.

2. There needs to be a personal organic or psychogenic problem.

3. It has to cause personal distress as evaluated on a personal distress scale questionnaire.

The Working Group For A New View Of Women's Sexual Problems headed by Leonore Tiefer, Ph.D., holds a more extreme position in opposition to the DSM-IV. Dr. Tiefer and her colleagues are concerned about what she calls "the medicalization of female sexual problems by urologists and the pharmaceutical industry." Much of what they advocate is in the context of victimization of women — their inequalities related to gender, class, sexual orientation, society, politics, and economy.

The Working Group On Sexual Problems has its own classification system for FSD.

I. Sexual Problems due to Socio-Cultural, Political, or Economic Factors.

II. Sexual Problems relating to Partner and Relationship.

III. Sexual Problems due to Psychological Factors.

IV. Sexual Problems due to Medical Factors.

Dr. Tiefer may be taking an extreme point of view for many admirable reasons, but treatment of FSD should not be an either-or situation. The qualified medical practitioner who treats FSD must never ignore the patient's socio-psychological background; nor should psychiatrists, psychologists, and sexologists who treat FSD ignore or trivialize potential or real organic causes of the patient's disorder.

If the reader wishes to learn more about Dr. Tiefer's views on FSD, please see Appendix B for contact information.

◆ ◆ ◆

It has been said of the medical profession that our knowledge of female sexual dysfunction is 20 years behind our understanding of male erectile dysfunction.

Therefore, all doctors first need to know the normative ranges of sexual function and sexual desire in women at all stages of their lives, especially during menopause and post-menopause. Of equal importance is how female sexual function changes from those norms during the different stages of a woman's life including both childbirth and menopause.

A woman is likely to have periods of lessened or lower feelings of sexual desire especially while pregnant and following childbirth. She and her partner should understand these changes, during which levels of sexual desire can rise and fall.

Normal sexual function is essentially a range, with no one single "correct" level and is always an individual issue. The availability of a partner and appropriate stimuli will affect a woman's normality. Intimacy is also an essential factor for a woman in a sexual relationship.

Early on, there may be intense desire due to the newness of the relationship, excitement of new discovery, that mindless first time in the heat of the moment, or blissful romance. Later, life's distractions and the personality of a woman's partner may have a negative effect on her sexual response. She may also have an increase in sexual desire as the relationship endures.

A woman's self-image is important at all stages of her life. So are levels of androgens, the hormones, which will affect her desire threshold. Taken together, all these complex factors underlie the difficulties of fully understanding the female sexual response.

TEN

Stages Of The Female Sexual Response

Despite the controversies over identifying and labeling the female sexual response, a vocabulary is necessary in order to understand female sexual function and as an aid in treating female sexual dysfunction.

Stage One of the female sexual response, *desire* or Libido, is a brain-controlled response, which can last from minutes to hours. Desire is effected by a number of factors that play an important role: Intimacy, knowledge, past experiences, prior trauma such as molestation, culture, religion, availability of a partner, and androgens. Without androgens, a woman may not be able to have an adequate sexual response.

Positive and negative influences from the brain ultimately control the genital response. Testosterone is responsible for programming these centers during prenatal life both in females and males, and in maintaining their sexual response.

Stage Two of the female sexual response is *arousal.* The duration can last from minutes to hours. According to the National Institutes of Health, an estimated 9.7-million women have self-reported complaints of this disorder.

During Female Sexual Arousal, sexual stimulation activates the central, parasympathetic nervous system, which leads to clitoral and vaginal smooth-muscle relaxation and increased genital blood flow (engorgement). Engorgement of the vagina and clitoris causes an increase in their diameter and length, lubrication, and a tenting of the upper half of the vagina.

Estrogen is responsible for maintaining normal vaginal health and for allowing lubrication. If there is low estrogen level such as occurs with postmenopausal vaginal atrophy (shrinking) or as a result of surgery, the arousal stage can be negatively affected.

At the female Arousal Stage, changes take place outside the genital-urinary tract such as an increase in heart rate, blood pressure, and muscle tension throughout the body. There is also enlargement and engorgement of the breasts, areolas, and nipples with nipple erection. As you might expect, the equivalent response in men would be erection.

The *sexual flush* is a skin (epidermis) reaction on the chest, neck, and face in about 75 percent of women experience during the Arousal Stage.

During the Third Stage of female sexual function, *orgasm*, a series of reflex or involuntary muscle contractions happen in the upper third of the vagina and pelvis, typically lasting 5 to 15 seconds.

Orgasm is usually the result of stimulation of sensory nerves, such as those located in the clitoris or possibly the G-Spot (or both) and other erogenous zones. The stimulation must be of adequate duration and intensity for the reflex of orgasm. It is primarily controlled by the sympathetic nervous system.

Orgasm is accompanied by contraction of muscle groups throughout the body, with an increase and intensity of heart rate, blood pressure, and respiration.

Female orgasm differs from male ejaculation/orgasm in that it has higher peaks and takes longer to reach the summit. Imagine, if you will, "The Big O" visually as Mount Everest compared to rolling green hills, although not necessarily as difficult to reach.

It is not unusual if a woman needs to "learn" how to reach orgasm, in essence to discover which foreplay is the catalyst, and that requires essential communication with her partner. Many women when making love can reach orgasm without penile penetration. Some experts have recommended specific pelvic and/or mental exercises (using the brain) as conditioning to reach orgasm.

Stage Four, *resolution*, lasts minutes to hours. In both women and men it is a sense of well-being, the "afterglow" of a couple's shared sexual experience. When extended, it intensifies the bond between partners, a *goal* for all couples in love to achieve and repeat on a regular basis.

FEMALE EJACULATION:

Many women report that during sexual stimulation and orgasm they experience ejaculation of a fluid from the urethra. Research has demonstrated, however, that this is not urine. Rather, it is a fluid high in fructose and thought to originate in the peri-urethral glands.

Unfortunately, a significant number of women have received the wrong medical diagnosis and have undergone needless surgery to "correct this problem" of wetting the bed during sex, not realizing, of course, that it is a natural phenomenon.

THE G-SPOT:

The Graffenberg or G-Spot is a sexually sensitive nerve intensive area on a woman's body inside the front wall of the vagina. It is usually located between the pubic bone and cervix, along the course of the urethra, near the bladder neck.

In some women, the G-Spot can be stimulated via pressure on the lower abdominal wall, above the pubic bone, just above the bladder. The actual G-Spot is often difficult to locate by touch, especially in the unstimulated state.

Unlike the clitoris, which is the major source of sexual stimulation in many women and the site of primary orgasmic reflex, the G-Spot may be part of the "vaginal" or secondary orgasmic reflex. Here, the G-Spot serves as a major source of sexual stimulation. During orgasm, this stimulation is transmitted via the pelvic nerves from the area of the G-Spot, causing rhythmic contractions in the muscles of the uterus and bladder, as well as the pubococcygeus ("PC") muscles.

In addition to the G-Spot's role in sexual pleasure, researchers, including Dr. Beverly Whipple, renowned author and sex researcher, have suggested that it also plays an adaptive role in women via a strong pain blocking effect, as seen during natural childbirth.

ELEVEN

Cultural Influences

Physicians and therapists should ascertain the role of cultural and orientation issues in a woman's life. Sexual behavior does differ throughout the world. In some societies marriages are still arranged. Some cultures are permissive, others brutally restrictive.

Because the United States has immigration from all over the world, we see partners from unassimilated ethnic groups who bring into their relationships varying cultural practices and expectations, which often contribute to FSD.

One of the most horrifying customs practiced *against* women is "female circumcision," defined by the World Health Organization as the deliberate removal or injury of the external female genitalia and organs for non-medical reasons. It is still practiced in parts of the Middle East and regions of Africa as a sanctioned practice and integral tradition that causes physical and psychological harm to young women.

A recent study reported that over 30 percent of married Egyptian women and more than 15 percent of their daughters have undergone this ritualistic mutilation.

Studies of women who underwent genital mutilation in early infancy, as compared to women who did not, have been shown to have significant differences in sexual function, including lack of libido and sexual satisfaction.

While most women reported it lessened sexual satisfaction, others firmly supported this practice. Those against female circumcision advocate education as a solution. Typically, women subjected to this procedure come from rural areas. The World Health Organization hopes to educate all and break the cycle of this barbaric ritual practice.

◆ ◆ ◆

Sexual satisfaction in lesbian relationships should also be considered since it has been reported that in general lesbian couples have less sex than heterosexual couples. The reasons for this are unclear, and it is probably dangerous to make generalizations. However, an intriguing thought suggests this possibility: Lesbian couples have the same amount of sex a heterosexual woman would have if she did not have to deal with her male partner's need for more frequent sex. But as in heterosexual relationships, sex is important for the lasting of the relationship. All biological and psychological issues that affect women and changes in their sexual function are applicable whether the woman is in same sex or heterosexual relationships.

PART III

CAUSES OF FEMALE
SEXUAL DYSFUNCTION

TWELVE

Categories Of FSD

As you might expect, there are several categories and degrees of Female Sexual Dysfunction. **Primary Sexual Dysfunction** is a condition in which sexual expectations have *never* been met. **Secondary Sexual Dysfunction** occurs when all stages of sexual function have been met in the past but the problem now exists. Studies in the early and mid-1990s showed that the prevalence of female sexual dysfunction is significant and associated with decreased desire, decreased vaginal lubrication, anorgasmia, and lack of pleasure.

Hypoactive Sexual Desire Disorder produces a deficiency in sexual fantasy or thoughts and/or desire or receptivity to sexual activity. Hypoactive female sexual desire disorder is quite common. Up to 50 percent of women with sexual dysfunction experience lack of sexual desire, which is a persistent or intermittent lack of sexual fantasies or interest in sexual activity. And this returns us to the question of what is basically *normal.*

Hypoactive Sexual Desire Disorder can be caused by problems in general health, hormonal imbalance, and medications, especially the anti-depressant medications that decrease libido. Also psychological and relationship issues can be involved in addition to family and job stress, aging, and menopausal changes. A loss of interest in sex and even fantasies may occur over the course of a long-term relationship. In addition, a number of women I have encountered who are divorced or widowed, with ages ranging from 40 to their 70s, freely admit they have little interest in having sex and can easily do without it. That may be the result of being without a partner for a long period of time.

One problem of FSD seen in women who have been in long-term relationships with impotent men is that they may display a low sexual desire over a period of time, which is often much more difficult to treat or reverse. This may in part be due to problems in communication with their partners. After a number of years, the partners may feel a certain level of comfort without sexual contact.

Another cause of low or no desire for sex might be sexual boredom within the partnership. Think of it this way: Even if chicken were your favorite food, would you want it served the same way every day? Probably not. However, the answer is not to look for a new chef, but rather a new "recipe" to incorporate change and variety *within* the relationship. Again, honest communication is the key.

Treatment will depend on the underlying etiology including lifelong problems, hormone disorders, chronic illnesses, and medications. Sex and couple therapy is often recommended for hypoactive sexual desire disorder and often has good success, especially if the onset of the problem is recent.

Sexual Aversion Disorder is persistent recurring distaste for sexual activity, with avoidance of genital contact. Although not as common as hypoactive sexual desire problems, Sexual Aversion Disorder is often accompanied by vaginal pain and may also be the result of past sexual or physical abuse or current relationship problems. While evaluation and treatment of any physical "pain" is the first step, individual or couple counseling may be very useful here. Conflict resolution of emotional problems need to be applied.

Female Sexual Arousal Disorder, FSAD, is a problem with the physical aspects of sexual excitement — lubrication, expanding of the vaginal opening, and the accompanying erotic sensations. A woman with FSAD may have sexual thoughts, but they are not communicated to her genitals, which manifests itself with lack of "subjective excitement" or genital lubrication. Some women who have FSAD are totally uninterested in sex; others enjoy contact only to a certain point with limits. Also, it can range from occasional to constant.

The inability or decreased ability for a woman to be aroused and/or lubricate during sexual stimulation is the most prevalent form of female sexual dysfunction and may be associated with menopause or other physical conditions including breast-feeding, reduced vaginal or clitoral blood flow, and diabetes.

Lack of vaginal lubrication may cause discomfort during intercourse, impairing a woman's feeling of arousal, which is then interpreted by her sex partner that she is not interested in sexual activity. While this is obviously not the case, it can lead to serious couples issues if communication is absent from the relationship.

The significant difference between women and men who have sexual dysfunction is "arousal". Most men with ED will have problems maintaining penile rigidity, complain of poor desire, *or* report difficulties with orgasm/ejaculation. In women SD is typically multi-dimensional, including problems of desire, arousal, *and* orgasm. However, even if the causes appear to be complex, one single organic answer to these problems in women is often evident: *insufficient androgens*, which will be discussed in subsequent chapters.

At a meeting of Urologists and Gynecologists in Boston that I attended early in 2000, we presented our evaluation of 37 women who complained of sexual arousal insufficiency and who had no history of systemic vascular conditions. They were ages 37 to 69, with a mean age of 56 years.

We evaluated them with a female arousal sexual questionnaire and looked at their cholesterol and triglyceride levels. Of note, 38 percent had *abnormal* lipid values diagnosed for the first time, and among these women the degree of SD was greater. Their propensity toward cigarette smoking was also noted, about 20 percent in both groups. Our study concluded that there is an important connection between systemic vascular risk factors, specifically high cholesterol levels and sexual dysfunction, especially in women over 40. We confirmed that female sexual arousal disorder may serve as a useful screening tool for vascular disease, and early evaluation may identify those women who are early candidates for heart attack or stroke.

Persistent Sexual Arousal Disorder, PSAD, is a recently reported female sexual disorder and is essentially the *opposite* of Female Sexual Arousal Disorder. PSAD is a disorder of unremitting sexual arousal characterized by physiological sexual arousal for an extended period of time. The symptoms do not ordinarily resolve with orgasm. It may even occur without sexual experience or desire. It can be triggered by either sexual activity or non-sexual stimuli. The overall physiological signs are persistent arousal that is *unwanted*. This may be similar to veno-occlusive priapism in the male (discussed in a later chapter). PSAD is not to be confused with the *myth* of nymphomania, also once referred to as sexual hyperaesthesia.

Female Orgasmic Disorder includes those women with decreased or inability to achieve orgasms. A surprising number have never experienced the sensation of orgasm; although women with "isolated" orgasm problems are a small percent of those with FSD. Usually orgasmic problems are part of desire and arousal dysfunction as well. Spinal injury, poor blood flow to the vagina or clitoris, surgical treatment in the past, genital trauma, and certain medications can wreak havoc on a woman's ability to reach orgasm.

Up to 10 percent of all women state they have never achieved an orgasm in any way. Many more report situational problems in which they have trouble reaching orgasm, typically during intercourse. Of note, only about 33 percent of women achieve orgasm with intercourse, typically because of no direct stimulation of or lack of penile contact with the clitoris. In addition, her partner's technique might be one of the causes. A recent study looking at the MRI (magnetic resonance imaging) of a couple engaging in sexual intercourse revealed the actual position of the penis in the vagina during copulation. At times there was a complete lack of clitoral contact, which confirmed earlier non-MRI studies. Like all forms of FSD, the inability to achieve orgasm, despite being sexually aroused, can be frustrating for both the woman and her partner.

If inhibited female orgasm is your problem, you still have reason to be optimistic. Once you have learned to reach orgasm, you probably will not lose that ability completely, unless medical problems, trauma, or personal relationship issues arise. Even then, you are more likely to recover that capacity in a short time

Recently, the condition of "Clitoral Phimosis" has been determined to be a common cause of female orgasmic disorder and will be addressed later in the section on specific causes of FSD.

6. Dr. Hakim's Waiting Room

Elizabeth turned away from Lauren and her eyes softened when a fit young woman sat on the other side of her with a chubby boy in her arms. "He's adorable."

"I know, and I'm waiting for the other shoe to drop. Terrible two's and all that."

Elizabeth had seen on Nova™ a documentary about male infants being born with genital problems. "Is he all right?"

"He isn't Dr. Hakim's patient, if that's what you thought. My babysitter wasn't available."

"What's his name?"

"Rodrigo. I'm Carmen."

"Elizabeth."

"Do you have children?"

"Not yet."

"Then are you seeing Dr. Hakim for fertility problems?"

"No, it's my first … our first visit to the doctor. My husband will be here in a while."

"Well, let me warn you about one thing when you do have children. Be aware you might be one of the twenty percent of women who don't regain their full sexual function after giving birth."

"That's why you're here?"

"Yes."

"What is it, postpartum depression?"

"No, hormonal problems, and it almost ruined our marriage."

"May I ask what happened?

"After giving birth to Rodrigo, I lost my desire for sex. Couldn't become aroused. Fortunately my obstetrician was familiar with that syndrome and recommended I see Dr. Hakim. My husband too. Dr. Hakim saved our marriage."

THIRTEEN

Pregnancy, Childbirth, Menopause and Hormonal Imbalances

Significant physiological events in a woman's life may affect her sexual function. During pregnancy, sexual activity may decline or increase depending on the trimester. The good news is that only a few medical restrictions might need to be imposed on couples who wish to have sex during pregnancy.

Of note, women who breast-feed their newborns may report decreased sexual desire and/or increase or change in coital pain on occasion. That is possibly secondary to changes in prolactin levels during lactation, which inhibits ovarian function, lowers testosterone and estrogen levels, lowers desire, and causes vaginal discomfort. Yet, a biologically driven peak of increased sexual desire in the pre-ovulatory cycle due to increased levels of testosterone may also occur.

Almost 40 percent of women during pregnancy have reported low sexual desire during the early trimester and from 3 to 6 months after delivery. The latter may be due to changes caused by labor, delivery, pain, low estrogen, and child-raising responsibilities. In fact, 1 in 5 women report decreases in sexual pleasure persisting after childbirth. Yes, *20 percent of women never recover full sexual function after childbirth.* Obviously this is a problem that can affect a pre-menopausal woman at any age and negatively impact her relationship with her husband or partner.

Men cannot really understand what childbirth does to the vagina. Trying to empathize or equate the same experience of pain and stretching, as happening to their own genitals is quite impossible. Imagine trying to pass a 10-pound kidney stone through the penis. Now you are beginning to comprehend what happens during childbirth.

Besides the attitudinal changes a woman goes through from pregnancy to the postpartum period, specific causes of her sexual dysfunction can result from injury or trauma during childbirth. Instruments such as forceps can cause scarring, neuromas, and sexual pain disorders.

A recent Boston study looked at postpartum sexual dysfunction amongst women over a 5-year period. In addition to the above, other causes of FSD included depression, physical exhaustion, lack of sleep, and other significant organic medical problems. This is obviously something that male partners need to be aware of and understand. Hormonal studies found that more than a year after childbirth, serum testosterone and DHEA levels were *low* in otherwise healthy women who had sexual dysfunction. This suggests that an *enzyme deficiency* may contribute to postpartum sexual dysfunction.

During menopause, primary ovarian failure causes decreased levels of estrogen and progesterone, resulting in cessation of menses. A recent study out of Australia looked at women's sexual functioning during the natural menopause transition. In late peri-menopause (less than 12 months into the menopausal cycle), the researchers saw a significant decrease in sexual responsiveness and overall sexual functioning, which affected the sexual performance of their partners as well.

Throughout the post-menopausal period, a further decline of female sexual responsiveness was noted, including decreased sexual activity, decreased libido, a significant increase in vaginal pain, and lack of lubrication. This also further impacted negatively upon both the partner's sexual performance and their mutual sense of well-being.

Other studies have also shown that there is a decrease in female sexual function during the menopausal period, suggesting a hormonal cause or hormone mechanism. However, we do not yet totally understand what is *normal*.

71

7. *Dr. Hakim's Waiting Room*

"Lauren, may I ask what caused your problem?" Elizabeth said when Carmen and her baby went into Dr. Hakim's examining room.

"I'm an avid cyclist. I started to experience clitoral numbness that lasted for several days after long mountain biking tours. The doctor concluded that a number of factors contributed to my sexual dysfunction, most notably my history of constant perineal pressure and injury due to bicycle riding. He said it's a well-documented sexual risk factor, especially in areas of arousal and orgasm."

"What is perineal?"

"That area between our anus and vagina. It contains a lot of tissues and arteries that deliver blood to our genitals. The bike seat compresses the arteries and nerves, it causes numbness and difficulty with arousal when I try to have sexual intercourse."

Elizabeth shuddered and on reflex crossed her legs. *"I never knew that sort of thing could happen. Glad I don't bike. So, what did the doctor advise?"*

"Well, first, he recommended I give up bike riding. But I really love it. It's a part of my life I wasn't willing to give up. So, he suggested I change bicycle saddles and use an anatomically friendly padded seat or reclining bicycle that doesn't put as much pressure on that region."

"Did it work?"

"After using my new bicycle seat for three months, I no longer experience clitoral numbness. I've also noted some improvement in my sexual function and found it's been easier to reach orgasm." Lauren stood up. "The nurse is calling me. Today I'm supposed to find out what happens next."

FOURTEEN

Illness And Injury

Spinal cord injury is an important area of concern. It is a serious problem that is often associated with various types of sexual dysfunction. Yet, some women with spinal cord injury may still experience genital sensation and have the capacity to stimulate vaginal blood flow and lubrication by masturbation.

Diabetes is a systemic disease that affects the vascular and nervous systems, as well as generating psychosocial effects. Validated studies show significant decrease in sexual function amongst women who are diabetic.

Symptoms include vaginal discomfort, vaginal dryness, lack of libido, poor clitoral sensation, difficulty reaching orgasm, all to a much higher degree when compared with age matched women who are not diabetic. Young women who experience the symptoms of SD may be getting an early warning. They would be well-advised to see their physicians and seek testing to learn if they are indeed diabetic or have some other significant medical problem.

Certain medical conditions such as **kidney disease** or **hypothyroidism** (underactive thyroid gland) can adversely affect a woman's sex drive. In addition, head injuries and neurological diseases such as **Parkinson's** and **osteoporosis** may be associated with FSD. Various surgical procedures such as **hysterectomy**, **abdominal perineal resection**, **radical pelvic surgery**, and major **vascular surgery** can have disastrous effects on a woman's sexual function as well.

Finally, studies have suggested that exposure to occupational or environmental toxins such as lead, mercury, and vinyl chloride can affect sexual function.

Pelvic prolapse occurs when there is relaxation of the pelvic muscles that normally support the bladder, urethra, vagina, and rectum in their correct anatomic position. This can occur in women during menopause, after multiple childbirths, and with aging. The pelvic structures lose their supporting ability, and the pelvic organs begin to drop forming a hernia or bulge into the vagina or rectum or both. Common symptoms include urinary disorders such as incontinence, complaints of pain in the vagina and pelvic region, loss of sensation in the vagina and clitoris, and inability to achieve orgasm.

As in men, **blunt perineal injury** can lead to sexual dysfunction in women. To repeat, the perineal area is the soft tissue between the anus and vagina and includes the sexual organs and their associated neuro-vascular supply.

Perineal compression injury usually results from sports injuries, especially anatomically *hostile* bicycle seats. Various studies by Dr. Irwin Goldstein and his associates at Boston University Medical Center have proved conclusively that women can have SD secondary to sports injuries and bicycle riding. This research was done using physiologic testing of genital blood flow as well as vibratory and genital sensation. One particular study showed a significant decrease in clitoral and vaginal thermal (hot/cold) perception, and clitoral and labial blood flow. Sexually active women reported lack of sensation along the perineal region as well as numbness and bruising from their injuries and even bleeding on occasion. Evaluation and treatment by a qualified physician is imperative if you experience any of these symptons.

A major recommendation for bicycling enthusiasts is to use an anatomically friendly bicycle seat or sit in a reclining position if they choose not to abandon this activity.

Just Say "NO" to Narrow Bicycle Saddles!

FIFTEEN

Aging

The natural aging process in women may also contribute to any of the aforementioned categories of FSD: Disorders of desire, arousal, orgasm, and vaginal pain. Sexual dysfunction in older women is treated the same as in younger women: Identification, education, and modification.

A major factor in female sexual health is this: Up to 50 percent of women 65 and older have lost their partner, compared to only 14 percent of men in the same age group. Many women who still desire sex may not be active due to lack of a partner. Forget the myth as one ages desire for sex dwindles or disappears. The reality is this: As long as there is a loving relationship, sexual activity can remain pleasurable for couples at almost any age.

Older women who are divorced or widowed may need to become involved in activities that will allow them to meet potential partners. All women and men too should know as they age, it is even more important to be in optimum health to fully enjoy normal sexual activities. This includes good nutrition, maintaining an appropriate weight and cardiovascular and aerobic exercises, which not only makes people feel healthier and look better, it also improves their self-esteem.

Women who feel good and have a positive self-image will be better sexual partners. Remember, the ability to fantasize is important, and completely normal. Your fantasies increase arousal.

As women age, many will experience **vaginal dryness** and **atrophy**, which may require medical or hormonal therapy, lubricants, vibrators and other sexual aids to enhance the vaginal sexual response and experience.

Furthermore, as both partners age, their sexual response may be slower, and they may not focus on any specific sexual goal or performance to enjoy sexual activity. The older couple may achieve a more ideal attitude towards intimacy. Partners can express their affection to each other, touch each other, and feel good about each other even if their sexual goals may be different than when they were younger.

However, if the woman has difficulty with vaginal lubrication and/or the man has difficulty getting or sustaining an erection or reaching orgasm, specific treatments can certainly improve those functions. Although intercourse may not necessarily be a goal for every couple, it is certainly an activity that can be continued well into the "golden years."

8. Dr. Hakim's Waiting Room

"I couldn't help overhearing your conversation," a woman seated on the other side of Elizabeth said when Lauren left. "Everything she told you ... learning about her body is so true. I heard you give your name as Elizabeth. I'm Sonia."

Elizabeth guessed Sonia was in her late 40s or early 50s. "May I ask why you're here? Something to do with menopause?"

"Oh, no, not yet. I'm only forty-five. Essentially, I complained of depression to my primary care physician. She gave me an anti-depressant medication, Zoloft®, which was not successful. Then my psychiatrist treated me with Prozac®. Within two months of that treatment my symptoms of depression improved, but I also began to suffer severe anorgasmia."

"Is that what I think it is?"

"Yes, I could not reach orgasm. A lower dose of the medication didn't improve my sexual function. My physician sent me here to Dr. Hakim. My medical history showed no other problems. I'm not overweight. Dr Hakim explained how physical problems, such as clitoral phimosis, or an inability to expose the clitoris during sexual arousal can also cause anorgasmia. Thankfully, my exam showed I was normal in that area."

"Then it was only the medication?"

"Yes, Dr. Hakim told me that the various SSRI anti-depressants may often cause sexual dysfunction and difficulty achieving orgasm."

"What are SSRI anti-depressants?"

"Selective Serotonin Reuptake Inhibitors." Sonia showed Elizabeth her pills. "He recommended Buproprion® (Welbutrin SR) as a viable substitute medication. It controls depression with-

out causing sexual dysfunction. Since my hormonal tests were normal, he also told me if Buproprion wasn't successful, I could take sildenafil ... that's Viagra ... in doses up to 100 mgs."

"Viagra works for women too?"

"Yes, I've been told if your hormone levels are normal, it can be effective in restoring normal sexual arousal in women. But so far, I don't need it. That's why I'm here today, to have another checkup and tell the doctor I'm staying on Buproprion. It's controlling my depression without any negative side-effects. Elizabeth, it's like having a new lease on my sex life!"

SIXTEEN

Depression

Depression is a major risk factor for SD and may be associated with chronic illness. Various questionnaires such as the Beck Inventory for Depression can be useful in evaluating a woman's history before she is offered treatment.

All too often, women with classic symptoms of FSD — lack of desire, arousal, sensation, ability to have orgasm — are misdiagnosed as having *depression,* when instead they are experiencing hormonal problems leading to FSD and are placed on anti-depressant therapy. Unfortunately, common anti-depressant drugs, such as the SSRI, Selective Serotonin Reactive Inhibitors, can cause sexual dysfunction in both men and women, or make it worse.

If these women are fortunate to see a specialist in FSD, this problem can be recognized, and they can be treated successfully with other agents, such as hormonal therapy or sildenafil. In fact when many of these women were put on these agents, a number found that they no longer needed antidepressants, and were indeed much happier because their sexual function had returned or improved.

Medications, including various anti-hypertensives (high blood pressure) and tranquilizers, can also decrease sexual desire and cause SD.

For those suffering from depression and who want their sexual functioning restored, multiple therapies have been utilized with alternate antidepressant medications such as Buproprion, which has been quite effective. It successfully treats their depression and in many cases restores sexual function. Additionally, the use of sildenafil (Viagra) has been effective in certain individuals on anti-depressant medications with a *normal* hormonal status.

Anti-psychotic drugs can also cause orgasmic problems. Illicit drugs, barbiturates, and marijuana can cause FSD. They are often under-recognized and under-reported and affect essentially the libido and ability to achieve orgasm.

Of interest, certain SSRI drugs given in low doses are used successfully to treat *premature* ejaculation in men. These agents can delay ejaculation and time to orgasm, which prolongs satisfaction for both partners. However, higher doses can result in an inability of both sexes to achieve orgasm.

9. Dr. Hakim's Waiting Room

Lauren returned to the waiting room with a big smile on her face and went over to Elizabeth. "I'm going to be okay, back to normal in a few months, the doctor says, provided I use an anatomically friendly bicycle seat."

"That's great."

"We'll be in touch?"

"I'll call you tomorrow and let you know what the doctor told me."

Lauren flashed a reassuring smile. "I'm sure everything'll turn out okay."

After Lauren left, Elizabeth tried to read one of the office magazines, but she repeatedly glanced at her watch as she worried if Brad would show up. Also, two women were speaking loud enough for her to hear, and she found their conversation interesting.

" ... and so, Cory, I made it to age 38 with no complaints of sexual dysfunction. Then I had an accident that caused blunt trauma to my vagina. Since then, I've experienced clitoral pain and inability to reach orgasm when my husband and I have intercourse."

"What are you doing for it, Olivia?"

"Oh, I tried multiple vibrators and manual stimulation, but the severe pain doesn't allow me to reach orgasm during sexual activity. On top of that, I recently had a hysterectomy, which has led to decreased arousal. Thank God, the surgeon left my ovaries in place and my hormone status is normal."

"Is your husband okay with it?"

"*Oh, it did affect his performance. Then Dr. Hakim's examination of my privates revealed that I had a* **neuroma** *... some kind of mass. After initial treatments with oral pain medications with no improvement in my clitoral pain, I started to receive steroid nerve blocks to the region of the pain. I'm here today for another treatment.*"

"*Is it working, Olivia?*"

"*I'll say! After a few treatments, my pain is almost gone, and things are just about back to normal.*"

SEVENTEEN

Vaginal Pain

Vaginal pain is a common manifestation of FSD. It is something that women do not normally talk about, and the symptoms may persist if left untreated. Studies have concluded that vaginal pain can be caused by scarring near the genital nerves, fibrosis, and neuroma (tumor or mass involving the nerves). Although the underlying cause is not always determined, it can also be a result of androgen deficiency.

Dyspareunia refers to mild-to-severe vaginal pain during sexual stimulation or sexual intercourse. The pain can be purely psychogenic, which means that it is caused by mental or emotional factors such as anxiety, fear of pain, depression, anger, or personal conflict. Or, it can stem from a physical condition such as an infection of the vagina or urinary tract, PID (Pelvic Inflammatory Disease), poor vaginal lubrication, scar tissue in the vagina, neuroma, vaginal stenosis, endometriosis, menopause and low estrogen or androgen levels.

Dyspareunia also can be caused by shortening of the vagina after radiation therapy or surgery. In certain cases the exact location of the pain may not be discovered in women with long-term pain disorders and in certain situations empiric therapy, sexual therapy, or psychotherapy may be effective.

Treatment can include specific strategies aimed at the underlying cause. Various non-coital sexual techniques including manual or oral sex and change of positions during intercourse to decrease pain and sensitivity may be helpful. Additional therapies may include non-SSRI antidepressants to reduce chronic pain syndrome and specific techniques to reduce anxiety.

Regardless of the cause for dyspareunia or vaginal pain, a careful physical examination is critical to try and locate the exact area of the pain.

Vulvar Vestibulitis, a localized inflammatory process of a woman's genitalia can be a significant cause of pain and disability in women. A physician can make this diagnosis and offer treatment.

Vaginismus is a disorder involving recurrent involuntary spasm of the outer portion of the vagina during intercourse, which makes penetration painful and even impossible. Among some women, these contractions can even occur in the beginning stages of sexual arousal.

Like dyspareunia, vaginismus can be caused by psychological factors, such as the anticipation of pain. It can be caused by stress in the relationship and/or other psychological problems such as sexual inhibition, a history of trauma such as abuse or negative experiences with a previous or current partner. However, any woman suffering from vaginismus should be aware that her dysfunction might also be caused by physical or anatomical factors such as infection or endometriosis, which must be clearly identified and treated.

Treatment of vaginismus has typically involved the use of hormones, sex therapy and graduated dilators with relaxation techniques. The latter ultimately involves the woman's partner, who slowly inserts his penis by degrees under her guidance and control.

EIGHTEEN

Cancer and FSD

BREAST CANCER:

Each year, over 200,000 women are diagnosed with breast cancer. Multiple studies have shown breast cancer may lead to all types of sexual dysfunction and decrease in sexual satisfaction during and after treatment.

Breast cancer can have a long-term negative effect on sexual function of women and last long past the survivor's treatment. Surgery may result in many problems, as can post-operative radiation and chemotherapy. All can affect a woman's sexual function through loss of esteem, poor body image, lack of energy, depression, and anxiety regarding her partner.

Although there is improvement after treatment, a woman's sexual function may not return to pre-cancer levels even after two years. Studies have shown that Female Sexual Dysfunction is also related to the length and type of breast cancer treatment, such as radiation and chemotherapy.

Ideally, questions relating to sexual function should be asked early on, even before treatment begins, although prolonging one's life takes precedence and concerns about sexual function are often not considered at that time. If you are undergoing any of those treatments for breast cancer, you should ask your physician about the side-effects that could negatively impact your sexual function.

GYNECOLOGICAL CANCER:

Radical surgery for gynecological cancer can cause nerve damage and shortening of the vagina, and radiation therapy can worsen symptoms of FSD both physically and psychologically, affecting body image and general self-esteem.

A woman may suffer loss of estrogen due to **oophorectomy** (removal of ovaries) and radiotherapy. Female Sexual Arousal Disorder, neurological impairment, and incontinence may also occur.

Gynecological cancer may require post-operative treatment for psychosexual problems as well. Treatments include anti-depressant medications, hormone replacement, sex therapy, and counseling for the couple to cope with the situation.

Treatment of **endometrial cancer** (uterine), which afflicts mostly post-menopausal women in their 60s, can lead to the same dysfunctions as gynecological cancer.

Ovarian cancer can appear at any age. Unfortunately diagnosis comes late for the majority of women; as a result, surgical and postoperative therapies are typically more aggressive. A woman's sexual function can also be affected due to harmful neurological side-effects, weight loss, pain, change of bowel function, loss of hair, issues of body image and self-confidence.

Vulvar and **vaginal cancer**, although less common, lead to the same effects of Sexual Dysfunction mentioned above. Invasive radical surgery, and significant surgical complications, as well adversely impact femininity and sexual function.

Hetero and same sex couples are equally affected. Cancer puts a strain on a couple's sexual relationship along with the life-threatening issue itself. Early rehabilitation and counseling may help restore some sexual function and sustain the couple's intimacy.

10. Dr. Hakim's Waiting Room

"Now let me tell you about my problems," Cory said to Olivia. *"I'm 50, married for 25 years. I've always enjoyed sex, but it hasn't been the same since I had an abdominal hysterectomy about 3 years ago."*

'Why did you need it?"

"Fibroids. My periods were painful ... impossible to bear sometimes. Now I'm experiencing diminished lubrication, which causes discomfort, even pain during sex. I'm also experiencing less sensation and, as the doctor puts it, muffled orgasms. As a result, my interest in sex has decreased while my 55 year old husband still has firm erections."

"Is this what I have to look forward to in 30 years?" Elizabeth said to herself.

Cory checked her watch. *"My husband should be here soon."*

"I thought you said he was okay."

"He is, but the doctor wants to speak with him anyway since Dr. Hakim said it's a "couple's disease". Besides, he's 55 and he hasn't been to the doctor in years. Aside from my medical history, physical exam, and lab tests, he wants us to receive a 'patient and partner education'. He recommended that I stop smoking, something he calls 'modification of reversible causes'. He's already recommended I try Viagra to increase my arousal, and something he calls the magic pill."

"Magic pill?" Cory exclaimed.

Elizabeth continued to listen to Olivia and Cory. *"At this rate,"* she told herself, *"I might end up learning more about my own body than I ever expected **before** I see the doctor."*

NINETEEN

Surgically Induced Menopause

Hysterectomy, the surgical removal of the uterus, can have significant adverse effects on a woman's sexual function. About 600,000 hysterectomies are performed each year. Those surgeries can cause all types of Female Sexual Dysfunction as a result of blood vessel and nerve damage, loss of testosterone and androgens, and psychological issues of well-being and self-image. Hysterectomies can damage the nerve and vascular supply to the vaginal smooth-muscle, which causes FSD. Unlike nerve sparing prostatectomies, as yet *no* nerve sparing hysterectomy has been proven consistently successful in preserving a woman's sexual function.

Recent studies have given us a better understanding of the female nervous system and autonomic enervation of the female pelvis area. As a result, more attention to nerve-sparing surgery has been suggested. By preserving the woman's nerve fibers, (as is performed in nerve-sparing radical prostatectomies in men), normal sexual function may be sustained post-operatively.

After hysterectomy, women may experience a dramatic decrease in their sexual arousal response. Sexual dysfunction as a result of surgically induced menopause obviously affects the quality of a woman's life, as well as that of her partner. Surgical menopause has the same effects as medical menopause, with or without oophorectomy, removal of the ovaries.

Sexual dysfunction manifests itself with the usual symptoms: Lack of desire, lack of arousal, painful intercourse, inability to achieve orgasm, general decreased responsiveness during sex, and decreased sensation.

Psychogenic side-effects also may occur in areas of self-image, lack of self-esteem, quality of life and overall sense of well-being.

The changes may be quite enormous at onset. Before undergoing surgery and ideally in the presence of your partner, you should thoroughly discuss with your physician all options and likely outcomes, including the effects of treatment and therapy on your sexual function.

Less invasive options may include endometrial ablation, which leaves part of uterus intact, and supracervical hysterectomy, which reduces interfering with the genital blood supply. Preservation of the cervix and upper vagina may result in maintaining sexual function by avoiding damage to certain nerves. Your doctor can discuss which is the most appropriate therapy for you.

◆ ◆ ◆

Loss of hormones results from surgically induced menopause, too. Estrogen deficiency can cause vaginal atrophy, poor self-esteem, anxiety, and short-term memory loss. Androgens come primarily from the ova-

93

ries. Their removal and radiation therapy may cause deficiencies that lead to low libido.

A study from Sweden appearing in the New England Journal of Medicine in May, 1999 reported on women who had cervical cancer and underwent treatments that caused changes in vaginal anatomy and function. The controlled study took place over a three-year period. Women who had cervical cancer ages 26 to 80 were compared against women without cervical cancer. They answered questionnaires about changes in their sexual function over those three years.

The treatment for an early diagnosis of cervical cancer in Sweden is surgery, with or without radiotherapy. The surgery performed was a radical hysterectomy with pelvic lymph node removal. Patients with metastasized lymph nodes were treated post-operatively with radiation; those without were treated with surgery alone.

The study showed that 68 percent of women who had cervical cancer and 72 percent of those who did not were still able to have regular vaginal intercourse. Twenty-six percent of those who had cancer had insufficient vaginal lubrication, compared to 11 percent of those without cancer. Twenty-six percent of those who had cancer and only 3 percent of those who did not reported a shortened, uncomfortable vagina. Twenty-six percent of those who had cancer and 4 percent of those who did not reported insufficient elasticity of the vagina. Twenty-six percent of those who had cancer reported moderate to great distress caused by vaginal changes as compared with only 8 percent of the control group. The frequency of orgasm and pleasure was the same in both groups.

The study also concluded that a significant percent of women who undergo treatment for cervical cancer will experience a change in vaginal sexual response, which leads to a decrease in sexual activity and considerable distress. The most common symptoms will be vaginal pain, lack of lubrication, and lack of vaginal elasticity.

Women should be more aware of these side-effects, discuss them with their physicians, and seek out the most effective treatments.

TWENTY

Androgens And Estrogens

As already mentioned, hormone levels definitely affect a woman's sex drive and sexual function. Changes in these levels occur throughout her menstrual cycle, while she is pregnant or breast-feeding, or before and after childbirth — essentially throughout her entire life. These changes can cause increased time to arousal, decreased vaginal and clitoral sensation, vaginal pain, and poor lubrication.

Although the exact role of androgens in a woman's sexuality is not fully known, we do know that they play major roles in her sexual function and dysfunction. They are essential in the normal development of female reproductive organs and sexual characteristics.

Androgens are steroid hormones produced by the gonads and adrenals, which are ultimately made from cholesterol. In post-menopausal women most of the sex steroids come from the adrenal via conversion of DHEA to testosterone, suggesting that active androgens can be made on demand.

Androgen insufficiency syndrome is a significant diagnostic challenge, and its diagnosis and treatment are not always clear. A significant question yet to be answered is how we would characterize normal healthy females in developing standards for androgen evaluation in general. Levels of what is normal and abnormal depend upon the varying standards of different laboratories as well as the patients' ages.

What is the "normal" range of androgens in a sexually healthy body? Not very specific. In men the normal range is from 500 to 2,000 units; in women it is much lower, in the 15 to 90 range.

Throughout the medical field, "normal" is developed by a "control" population (one without the disease). However, in both men and women it is not always easy to identify the population that has no sexual dysfunction within the group studied. So-called "normal" testosterone levels in women range from 15 to 90. Therefore, if a woman has a level of 25, she then is in the lower third of the population. That is where we look for existing FSD. In other words, we search the range of testosterone, not the absolute values.

Why do these women have androgen deficiency? One group includes women who have undergone hysterectomy (with removal of ovaries), prior chemotherapy, radiation treatments; another group includes women who use antidepressant drugs, birth control drugs, or even common OTC cold medications. These factors account for up to 10 percent of women with FSD.

We know that androgens play an important role in the normal function of the vagina. They affect arousal and orgasm because of sensation issues that are also androgen dependent. Even though these are complicated issues, a physician can often get to the bottom line of the dysfunction by replacing the androgens.

What about the other 90 to 95 percent of women who have androgen deficiency? We see a significant decrease in sexual desire in some women after childbirth. In fact, it has been suggested that one out of five women (20 percent) never recover full sexual function after childbirth. Why? There really is no relationship to the type of delivery, natural or C-section. Hormonal changes occur after childbirth as in post-menopausal women. So both pre- and post-menopausal women can have androgen deficiencies.

Regarding adrenal physiology and androgen production, the adrenal enzyme system is quite complex, and an enzyme can be missing, inactive or just not functioning. As a result, a woman with adrenal pathology can appear healthy and *still* have sexual dysfunction.

This may explain one reason for sexual dysfunction in women. In fact, every one of the adrenal enzymes and sex hormones are active from birth without cessation until time of death — with one exception. And that will be explained in the next chapter.

Of interest, recent studies at Boston University Medical Center evaluated pre- and post-menopausal women with SD. They found the majority had androgen levels in the lower third of what is currently considered *normal*. This androgen deficiency was "global"; it included testosterone, DHEA and DHEA-S.

These women were otherwise healthy, free of vascular disease. Most had symptoms of FSD for several years prior to participation in the study, and typically those symptoms were multidimensional. A high level of personal distress often resulted from their sexual dysfunction, followed by depression, which led to taking antidepressants and SSRI drugs that intensified the problem of FSD.

◆ ◆ ◆

Androgens not only play an essential role in desire and sensation, they also contribute to maximal smooth-muscle relaxation. The importance of androgens in allowing vaso-dilatation (widening of the arteries) and smooth-muscle relaxation in the vagina during the sexual response is a new concept and an important one.

The vaginal lining (endothelium) covers the vascular "bed". Vaginal lubrication is due to increased blood flow to that wall. However, all changes that occur, from blood flow to lubrication, are still being investigated.

One of the most important scientific findings to-date in the field of FSD is that the smooth-muscle within the vagina can be studied with chemicals and drugs to assess contraction and relaxation. An important discovery is that maximal vaginal smooth-muscle relaxation, which is thought to be necessary for *normal* sexual function, occurs in the presence of *androgens*, regardless of the vasodilator (stimulation) used. This is a critical point. We can see groups of women with all types of FSD and multi-dimensional sexual complaints, and in effect all problems, including lack of desire, can sometimes be ascribed to a *single* cause, **androgen deficiency**.

A normal ovary produces twice as much androgen as estrogen, which itself begins as an androgen. Loss of androgens during menopause develops more slowly than the relatively sudden loss of estrogen. Back in the 1950s, estrogen/androgen combinations were shown to improve female libido and a sense of well-being.

In the 1980s and 1990s studies showed increases of sexual motivation, greater desire, pleasure, and orgasm when menopausal women received estrogen and testosterone replacement therapy. A recent study from Massachusetts demonstrated that low libido and low levels of estrogen and testosterone in women typically appear around the age of 50. Some loss might happen in the years immediately preceding menopause as well.

◆ ◆ ◆

Often, post-menopausal women may experience biological changes. Vaginal atrophy can lead to loss of sensation and decreased self-image. Also already mentioned are decline and intensity of orgasm. Hormone therapy is useful in restoring those functions.

Although vaginal lubrication and vaginal wall thickness are androgen dependent, estrogen is also essential for maintaining pelvic blood flow and vaginal sensation. Primarily we see changes as a result of estrogen deficiency that can cause **vaginal atrophy**, which leads to sexual dysfunction.

What is vaginal atrophy? Blood flow to the vagina decreases, which causes lack of arousal and lubrication. The vaginal walls and lining become thin and the vaginal entrance becomes narrower. This can lead to problems with penile penetration, friction during intercourse, susceptibility to trauma, dryness, discomfort, and clitoral pain.

Post-menopausal estrogen deficiency can cause incontinence, pain, and general discomfort with urination as well as recurring urinary tract infections. All of this can result in loss of libido and interest in sex. Pituitary problems may also develop.

All of the above may negatively affect a woman's relationship with her partner, especially if communication is poor and they have been sexually active up to this time.

The good news is that estrogen deficiency can be successfully treated with estrogen replacement therapy.

Nitric Oxide Synthase (NOS) is an enzyme which has been found in the tissues of the vagina and clitoris. This important discovery concluded that nitric oxide — the critical Nobel Prize winning piece of the puzzle that led to the use of sildenafil/Viagra in men — also plays an important role in the control of blood flow in the vagina. Decreases in this enzyme result when estrogen is removed during menopause. This offers an important understanding of the cause of FSD in post-menopausal women. NOS has been shown to have some involvement in clitoral erection, and has been found in nerve fibers in the glans clitoris, suggesting a role for nitric oxide in the vaginal response. These findings may help explain why some women with FSD and a normal hormonal status may benefit from using sildenafil.

◆ ◆ ◆

Low androgen levels often contribute to FSD. In these cases, androgen replacement therapy will help cure those problems.

On a less romantic note, think of your body as a complicated machine. Both your body and the machine need a source of energy so that they may function properly. In a woman, one energy source in particular enables her to have a sexual response, and that is ANDROGENS. Without them her "engine" simply may not function. Truly amazing and perhaps unbelievable, many women simply do not have sufficient androgens to allow normal sexual function.

Studies suggest that a significant number of women have chronically decreased libido when their testosterone and DHEA blood levels are below those of non-menopausal female controls. Female genital response during sex is often directly related to testosterone levels. Although testosterone is normally seen in concentrations 10 to 50 times less in women when compared to that of men, it, nevertheless, plays a very important role in female sexual function. This is especially important when considering therapy for FSD.

Testosterone levels have been measured *during* the menstrual cycle. Some researches think that the highest levels are seen in the middle third of the cycle — the time of ovulation and maximal fertility, which, although desirable, is still controversial.

Yes, testosterone is involved in the sex drive of *both* women and men. In their 30s and 40s, women experience a 15 percent drop in testosterone levels. Removal of the ovaries, often a part of hysterectomy, can reduce production to near zero.

As with other androgens, testosterone enables genital smooth-muscle relaxation, which allows for a normal sexual response. Scientifically speaking, low testosterone levels in women negatively affect the smooth-muscle of the clitoris and vagina leading to decreased inflow of blood, poor or no clitoral engorgement and decreased arousal.

Testosterone or **Androgen Deficiency Syndrome** is often seen in women with FSD problems. Some may be pre- or peri-menopausal, others post-menopausal. Various studies have looked at these effects and have shown that low testosterone levels and decreased libido can occur at all stages of a woman's life, *even as early as her teenage years.*

NOTE: Oral contraceptives *may* contribute to lowering levels of testosterone in women, which can diminish their sex drive, and this should be discussed with the physician who prescribes them.

DHEA, DHEA-S, and other adrenal gland hormones as they relate to sexual function are still being investigated by traditional medicine. DHEA has been used for years by the alternative medical community as an anti-aging hormone and is known as the "master hormone" because it is a precursor, or "parent", of estrogen, estradiol, progesterone, testosterone, and other sex steroids. DHEA is an important part of the link to normal female sexual function and its restoration. Recently it has gained heightened interest as a catalyst for female sexual thoughts, fantasies, desire, and activity.

In summary, *lack of androgens is a key factor in causing female sexual dysfunction. Their role is truly amazing.* However, while female sexual desire is related to androgens, *always remember that other factors also play a part* — including poor communication with your partner, history of sexual abuse, and lack of knowledge, to name a few.

PART IV

MANAGEMENT OF FEMALE SEXUAL DYSFUNCTION

TWENTY-ONE

Taking The First Step

Are you sexually active? Do you have any questions or concerns about your sexual health? Then talk to your physician! That may be all you need to start the conversation, which can then lead to successful treatment of any problems.

The longer you delay reporting your sexual dysfunction, the more difficult it is to treat. You must speak with your physician about it as early as possible.

Typically, individuals have great difficulty first admitting and confronting their problem of sexual dysfunction, communicating with a partner about it, and then making that first visit to a gynecologist, urologist, or other sexual medicine specialist.

For women, I would advise *them* to speak about it with their gynecologists (usually their primary physicians) for one very good reason. I have lectured all over the world, and each time, I ask the women in the audience to raise their hands if their primary care physicians or gynecologists have ever asked them about their sexual functioning. Almost always, not a single hand is raised. Remember, the burden is on *you* to bring up the topic with your doctor. Anecdotally, many women in their 20s who are taking oral contraceptives will say that their physician never mentioned the possible side-effects of decreased desire and libido, or even that young women can have sexual problems.

As has been stated repeatedly, any form of sexual dysfunction may be the first symptom of *something else* that may be physically wrong. Female or male, whenever you undergo a routine physical exam, your primary care physician should ask you if you have had any form of SD in the past or if you are experiencing it now. Then your doctor should explain that SD is very common and ranges from mild to severe, that it can often be reversed or prevented, and certainly can always be treated to allow for a more enjoyable sex life.

At least 30-40 percent of the time, a woman's husband or male partner has a problem too. If she has a female partner, that percent might be higher.

The approach to curing FSD is threefold:

- Identification of the cause.

- Education about risk factors, and modification.

- Intervention.

Many women, some as early as their teens, see their OB/GYN regularly for oral contraception pills. Later their visits to the doctor will include issues of childbirth, change of life, and aging. These are excellent times to discuss with a physician your sexual history and function.

Your doctor should ask you: Is your sexual dysfunction a new problem? When did it begin? Is it chronic, due to poor relationships or emotional conflicts?

Your physician should also ask about a history of incest, sexual abuse, trauma, molestation, or even rape. If these are found then appropriate counseling should be arranged.

In addition, the *sexual expectations* of you and your partner should be assessed. Relationship issues such as social and job stress also need to be evaluated as they may cause anxiety and FSD.

◆ ◆ ◆

Recognize that most physicians are not well trained when it comes to dealing with female sexual dysfunction disorders. So, let's discuss the role of the *physician* in the context of female sexual health.

Most physicians have not demonstrated an interest in female sexual health. Too many doctors tend to freeze and ignore complaints of FSD. They often put off their patients by telling them it is an acceptable part of the aging process or suggesting it is purely psychological. FSD is like any other *disease* and questions must be asked. Even if they are not trained in this area, physicians still need to inquire and at the very least recommend a specialist in the field of sexual dysfunction.

Yes, typical reasons why you will not be asked about your FSD, or have your complaints quickly brushed aside by your doctor, include little time available in our world of HMOs, poor patient/physician interaction, lack of knowledge, and their emotional discomfort. Regarding the latter and based on my experience, both female *and* male doctors are often too uncomfortable to inquire about and pursue patient's complaints of SD.

Yet, I believe that your doctor has an *obligation* to inquire, diagnose, prescribe, and help prevent and cure any problem of FSD. Since her physician is often the first individual whom women will confide in about her SD and other sexual issues, they may discover other undiagnosed health problems presenting themselves first as FSD. Women need to treat any physical problem in the context of their personal lifestyle, and other relationship issues.

Many people will already have had their heads filled with misinformation (or misunderstood information) from TV talk shows, ads for treatments, and non-validated surveys in pop-culture periodicals. Their doctors should explain which are facts, which are half-truths, or which are outright fiction.

Be secure that the FDA has approved effective treatments for various sexual dysfunction disorders. FDA studies and recommendations should be part of your evaluation.

Your primary care physician may send you to a gynecologist or urologist to deal with your Female Sexual Dysfunction. The specialist will first want to know your medical, sexual, and social history to rule out any psychological cause. Then you may be asked to fill out one of the validated sexual index questionnaires. After consultation, you can expect assorted medical tests and lab studies to help better define the problem prior to therapy.

Remember, SD is a *disease*, a *couple's disease*, and the cause needs to be understood prior to selecting the appropriate treatment for you. It is up to you, the patient, to bring this up to your doctor if the right questions are not even asked. Only by taking control over your own sexual health will you be able to improve your sexual satisfaction.

TWENTY-TWO

The Role Of Diagnostic Questionnaires And Medical Histories

Your physician may give you a "Female Sexual Dysfunction Questionnaire" (FSDQ) to fill out prior to treatment. Many have been and are being developed to examine changes in sexual function as perceived by the patient. These questionnaires help the physician understand the dysfunction and may serve as a baseline prior to therapy. The degree of personal distress caused by sexual dysfunction in a woman is also an important factor in the evaluation and diagnosis.

The Index of Female Sexual Function (IFSF) developed by Rosen in 2000, and the Brief Index of Sexual Function for Women (BISF-W), are two of the most commonly used indices of FSD. The IFSF is a scale used by both researchers and physicians to evaluate the degree of sexual dysfunction in women and has been validated by a large number of control-based studies.

The BISF-W is a self-reported inventory of sexual interest, activity, satisfaction, and preference. This questionnaire is validated, highly reliable, and distinguishes between depressed women and sexually dysfunctional, mentally healthy patients reflecting their sexual experiences.

The Female Sexual Distress Scale is a useful diagnostic tool and gives a perspective on the impact of personal distress caused by a woman's FSD. For instance, if an individual woman is *not* experiencing personal distress, then treatment may not even be necessary. The physician also needs to know if the patient's sexual problems are recently acquired or lifelong, global or situational.

Another validated questionnaire used to identify the specific area of a woman's sexual dysfunction is the Arizona Sexual Experience Scale (ASES). It is based on control studies of women with and without sexual dysfunction. The ASES demonstrates internal consistency, test and retest reliability, and general usefulness in identifying somebody suffering from sexual dysfunction. The woman is asked to respond to five questions based on her experiences of the past week including the day she answers the questionnaire. It is a reliable and simple instrument to help assess the cause of the sexual dysfunction.

Along with honestly answering the questionnaires, you must describe the problem to your doctor. Your physician should be a good listener and ask the following: When did your FSD begin? How long has it been going on? What other factors worsen or relieve the problem? Your physician should also seek truthful answers to modifiable social factors and issues that can impact your life such as smoking, alcohol, drugs, and stress.

You should be able to answer the most personal questions. How do you feel about your dysfunction? How does FSD affect your lifestyle? Were you sexually abused as a child? Did your FSD develop after childbirth? Do you have enough time for yourself to eliminate stress? Have you communicated your FSD to a regular partner or are you keeping it to yourself? Are you too tired to have sex?

Where and at what point does it hurt? Are you able to orgasm? When? Not at all? Do you masturbate? How often? Is your FSD a problem of libido? Was it a sudden or gradual onset?

These and similar questions help the doctor understand their effect on both you and your partner.

◆ ◆ ◆

Next, your doctor should take a detailed medical history. Often, this reveals the underlying problems and risk factors that explain why you are experiencing FSD. Important risk factors include the presence of diabetes, high cholesterol, certain medications, prior surgery, and a heart condition.

Your physician will look at multiple factors that may very well impact on your sexual functioning. They include menstrual cycle, single versus multiple partners, endocrine or hormonal imbalance, effects of the "pill", depression, pelvic surgery, radiation treatment for cancer, multiple sclerosis, diabetes, trauma to the genitalia, and spinal cord injury.

Also, be sure to tell your doctor about any medications you might be taking. Antidepressants, anti-psychotics, blood pressure medications, and chemotherapeutic drugs may affect your sex drive, decrease arousal, and delay orgasms. In certain cases it may take longer and more intense foreplay for arousal to occur.

Various medications are more likely to cause FSD than others. You should be reminded that anti-depressant agents, such as the SSRI drugs, have been shown to contribute to sexual dysfunction. They can significantly delay the time it takes to reach orgasm and lower sexual pleasure. Other classes of antidepressants may have less negative effects on sexual function. For example, Buproprion may be a viable alternative, but first consult your physician.

Your physician should also look for vascular problems, obesity, recent changes in weight, and ask about which "over-the-counter" (non-prescription medicines) cold and herbal remedies you take. You may well be surprised that certain OTCs may cause FSD.

Remember that sex is a partnership. These complete evaluation studies must deal with a woman's sex partner. Bear in mind that male or female, your sex partner may also be experiencing some form of SD.

11. Dr. Hakim's Waiting Room

"She's younger than I am!" Elizabeth said to herself when a couple entered the waiting room and sat opposite her. The girl looked like a high school student, petite and trim in white T-shirt and jeans, although she wore a wedding band. Her husband, whose shirt advertised Jim's Pest Control, was mid-twenties, she guessed.

The couple seemed happy and laughed together as they turned the pages of one of the office magazines. Then the young woman made eye contact with Elizabeth. "Hi, I'm Emma Sue," she said with a North Carolina Mountain accent.

"Elizabeth."

"Your first time here, isn't it?"

"Yes, how could you tell?"

"Oh, we've been seeing Dr. Hakim for almost a year now, so I can pretty much get a read on people." She got up and sat next to Elizabeth. "Care to tell me why you're here?"

Elizabeth briefly summarized her problem with Brad. "And why are you seeing the doctor?"

Emma Sue took out her wallet and showed Elizabeth photos of four children. The oldest looked about five or six, the youngest no more than a year old. "Aren't they just the cutest?"

"Adorable, but you look so young to have had four children," Elizabeth said.

"Well, I am 22. Got married when I was 16. Had my four beautiful babies, and would you believe ... I'd never experienced an orgasm."

"What?"

115

"It's the truth. And I'd been watching all those TV talk shows where the experts talk about female issues, sex, even our favorite, Howard Stern, when it suddenly hit me. My gynecologist never asked me about my sex life. I went to her for a total physical, and she found nothing wrong with me. Never examined my clitoris either ... and she should've. Then in the car, I heard Dr. Hakim on the radio, made an appointment, and within minutes of my physical found the problem."

"Which was?"

"When Dr. Hakim gave me my physical, he noticed that the hood of the skin over my clitoris couldn't be retracted or pulled back. It was stuck! He called it clitoral phimosis and explained that it wasn't uncommon in women with my complaint."

"What can be done about that?"

"Topical estrogen therapy. I rub the stuff on my clitoris. It allows the foreskin to be more pliable. My clitoris is more exposed now during sexual stimulation. At least the doctor didn't have to cut it open."

Elizabeth shuddered. "And now do you reach orgasm?"

"Do I ever! Can you believe it? I had to have four babies before I learned that I could really enjoy sex! I never realized how great sex with my Jimmy could be. I really look forward to it now ... especially whenever we can get my mom to watch the kids."

TWENTY-THREE

The Physical Exam And Lab Tests

After evaluating your sexual, social, and medical histories, your specialist will give you a comprehensive physical examination, including a pelvic and genital exam, and order certain lab tests. In many cases of FSD, such exams and tests will uncover an underlying *organic cause* of your problem.

While in men the physical exam primarily focuses on one organ, in women a number of defined sex organs are involved. These can affect sexual function and must be examined and evaluated *completely*.

The start of your physical begins typically with height and weight measurements, the taking of blood and urine samples. If you are severely underweight, especially anorexic, your menstrual cycle may be affected, or it may even indicate thyroid problems. Skin changes may be a sign of diabetes.

You will undergo a breast examination to rule out any masses or tenderness. However, if you have received a recent Pap smear and breast exam from your gynecologist, the sexual dysfunction physical will begin with an external examination of your genitalia followed by internal examination, especially if you have problems with vaginal pain.

During the normal examination of the clitoris, digital upward displacement of the labia by the physician should allow full retraction of the clitoral prepuce or foreskin to enable complete exposure of the glans. Everything should be explained during the procedure and with a mirror so you can see and understand what the doctor is doing. Topical agents can be used to increase swelling of the labia for purposes of the examination.

Your physician will examine you, looking for any abnormalities and to see if the tissues are pink and healthy. The doctor will also look for any involuntary vaginal contractions, vaginal discharge problems, and evidence of vaginal atrophy.

On internal examination, any pain can indicate an infection, inflammation or other genital and cervical diseases, including PID, vulvar vestibulitis and ovarian disease.

One abnormality that may be seen is a **clitoral phimosis** (See Figure), a condition in which the prepuce (hood) covering the glans clitoris cannot be fully retracted to expose the clitoris during sexual arousal. Clitoral Phimosis ranges from incomplete foreskin retraction and limited exposure to complete, with all stages in between.

Clitoral Phimosis may cause anorgasmia (inability to achieve orgasm) due to insensitivity and lack of exposure of the clitoris during direct sexual arousal — manual, oral, or penile.

Studies by the aforementioned Dr. Irwin Goldstein have shown that clitoral phimosis can be seen in up to

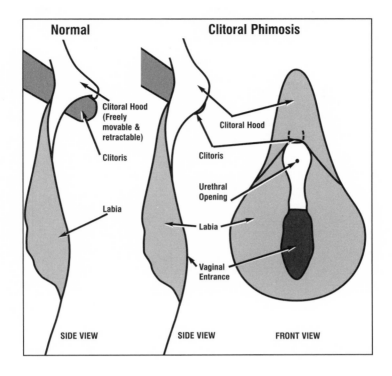

25 percent of patients with FSD. The physical abnormality is graded from 1 to 3 in severity.

This interesting physical finding is similar to phimosis in the male penis where a tightened foreskin prevents exposure of the penile glans.

The vast majority of women with clitoral phimosis will have poor orgasm sensation. Often times, these women will see many doctors over the years before the problem is diagnosed, so patients must be aware about this possibility.

Clitoral phimosis can also be due to **lack of androgens** or **estrogens**, which affects genital tissue health. Treatment of clitoral phimosis with topical estrogen or with surgery in some cases may in fact help these women to achieve orgasm and sexual satisfaction.

◆ ◆ ◆

The bimanual exam is essential to rule out any masses or tenderness. Evaluation for the presence of prolapse or urinary incontinence is also performed.

A rectal examination is necessary as well, assessing for normal sphincter tone, pain, masses, or blood.

As women age, they may have some complaints at the various stages of their sexual response, which can be brought on either by natural menopause or surgical menopause due to hysterectomy or oophorectomy. Many sexual complaints of women are not psychological. They are related primarily to *decreased genital blood flow or sensation,* many of which can be traced in part to androgen insufficiency.

One of the problems to overcome in the successful diagnosis of a patient's FSD is accurately quantifying the female sexual response. Some of the prescribed methods for evaluating female physiological changes include FSD questionnaires, tests for arousal and vaginal engorgement, and measuring vaginal labial temperature changes and pelvic contractions.

Other parts of the exam may include specialized non-invasive physiologic testing.

Vaginal pH testing gauges normal arousal. An increase in the vaginal pH during sexual arousal may help ensure sperm survival for procreation as opposed to the more acidic pH found in a non-aroused vagina.

Duplex Doppler Ultrasonography with visual sexual stimulation or pharmacologic stimulation measures vaginal and clitoral blood flow, as engorgement is essential to enhancing sexual activity and enjoyment. The velocity of clitoral blood flow ranges from 50 to 70 centimeters a second in contrast to only 30 to 40 centimeters per second in the male cavernosal arteries. The use of Duplex Doppler Ultrasonography is successful in measuring clitoral, vaginal, labial, and urethral arteries, in other words, total female genital hemodynamics during sexual arousal. It is a successful diagnostic tool because all measurements of blood flow responses are in "real time" and can be measured dynamically.

Hence measuring female hemodynamics after stimulation is an effective physiologic test to evaluate female sexual arousal. In addition, changes in vaginal lubrication, elasticity, and compliance can also be measured.

Vibratory Perception Measurements (Biothesiometry) tests how the woman reacts to a vibratory probe placed in the genital area and can be used to objectively document sensory function within the genitals. The clitoris contains a large number of densely packed sensory receptors that pass from the dorsal clitoral nerves to the genital nerves and spinal cord. All those receptors are **androgen dependent**. Many women with neurologically based FSD are not suffering from MS or injuries; they lack sufficient androgen.

Biofeedback may be a useful adjunct in the woman's physiologic evaluation, which can help her visualize the changes in her genital blood flow and receive information about the physiologic basis of the problem.

◆ ◆ ◆

Lab tests are geared for the individual woman to help find the underlying cause of her SD and may reveal organic causes of her FSD. Important are blood count for anemia, hormone levels for androgen insufficiency, which may be associated with depression and decreased libido, blood glucose for diabetes, lipid panels for high cholesterol (hypercholesterolemia), and thyroid function tests for any thyroid abnormalities. All can be treated.

The biochemical profile is useful to evaluate kidney and liver function. Urinalysis is important too for it can reveal evidence of infection. Below is a list of commonly prescribed lab tests.

Recommended Lab Tests For FSD Evaluation
CBC
Testosterone (total/free)
Serum glucose
DHEA
DHEAS
Estradiol
FSH
LH
Prolactin
Androstenedione
LFTs (Liver Function Tests)
TFTs (Thyroid Function Tests)
Urinalysis
SHBG (Sex Hormone Binding Globulin)

Depending upon the patient's history, physical findings, and laboratory evaluation, further clinical studies may then be recommended. Appropriate treatment depends on the causes of the patient's SD. Screening for chronic or life-long illnesses, including hormone or endocrine disorders, is important and essential.

More than 50 percent of all women may suffer some form of sexual dysfunction during their lifetime, and for many, the cure may come down to a single *magic* pill. The vast majority of women experiencing SD can be treated successfully.

◆ ◆ ◆

IN THE IMMEDIATE FUTURE:

At this time, new technologies are being developed and utilized for the evaluation of FSD. Functional Magnetic Resonance Imaging (MRI) of the brain has recently been reported as a useful tool to evaluate the female sexual arousal response. Therefore, MRI is emerging as an important tool in evaluating the brain and central nervous system as it relates to FSD.

A recent study from Korea reported that MRIs of healthy women helped demonstrate and evaluate brain activity during sexual visual testing.

Current research being done in France studied MRI visualization of sexual intercourse. It was the first time this study has been done. The MRI was performed while a volunteer couple was having sexual intercourse. It showed the anatomical comparison between "missionary" and rear entries to the vagina.

The study concluded that there is a difference in stimulation between the two positions. Thus the pleasures felt and experienced may also differ. No direct clitoral contact was demonstrated, however, possibly explaining why many women fail to achieve orgasm during intercourse.

FSD experimental evaluations include a diagnostic test known as **vaginometry** used to measure vaginal anatomy and compliance and diagnose conditions of FSD. Vaginometry is performed with a vaginal pressure balloon. It is inserted, filled slowly, allowing vaginal volume, compliance, and elasticity to be measured at varying pressures. Typically, vaginal volumes in post-menopausal women were shown to be lower and have less compliance than in pre-menopausal women. This type of evaluation is important because the shape, angle, and length of the vagina may be important with regard to sexual function, response, and decrease of pain.

Another evaluation tool being looked at by research institutions is the Thermal or Small Fiber Perception Testing of FSD, which utilizes a form of neurosensory analyzer to evaluate thermal or temperature perception and therefore neurologic function. Remember, sensory receptors are **androgen dependent.**

A recent Boston University Study showed that abnormalities in general sensitivity and peripheral nerve sensitivity were identified in women with FSD. In addition, the use of thermal/small fiber testing as a qualitative tool allows for a standardized method of evaluating the clinical course of those treated for sexual dysfunction.

All in all, women can look forward to a future in which more effective evaluation techniques, therapies, and devices will be available to diagnose and treat their sexual dysfunction.

TWENTY-FOUR

The Role Of Sexual Therapy

After all tests are completed and analyzed with your medical, sexual, and psychosocial histories, your physician will have a comprehensive physiologic and objective understanding of your sexual dysfunction.

While similarities in the development and sexual response of women and men do exist, the female sexual response is more often multi-factorial and distinct from that of the male. That is why we should not treat a woman's FSD in the exact same way as we do a man's ED. Pharmaco-therapy or other organic treatments *alone* are effective for *men* most of the time.

The context in which a woman experiences sexuality is just as important, if not more so, than the physiological outcome. Her emotional and relationship issues need to be addressed prior to beginning any medical therapy.

Even if a physical or organic condition is causing a woman's sexual dysfunction, important psychosocial and interpersonal relationship factors are often associated with her problem. For this reason, it may be difficult to treat a woman with medications alone if she has, for example, sexual arousal disorder. In most cases of physiologic FSD, pharmaco-therapy should be combined with some form of sexual therapy and even couple's counseling in certain cases to maximize satisfaction.

It cannot be emphasized strongly enough, however, that the woman should include her partner when seeking evaluation and treatment of her sexual dysfunction. *Sex is a partnership, and sexual dysfunction is a couple's disease.*

Your physician and your sex therapist should recommend specific lifestyle changes, such as:

- Stop smoking.

- Cease or moderate your alcohol consumption.

- Lower your cholesterol.

- Select a healthier diet.

- Reduce stress.

- Exercise regularly.

- Prioritize your relationship with your partner.

- Vary your sexual activities with your partner.

- Do not let child rearing obliterate your sex life.

These suggestions and more are covered in greater detail in Chapter Fifty-five.

Various psychological factors resulting from social and cultural issues, family ties, and an inability to enjoy sex may play a role in causing FSD. Other issues include a feeling of total responsibility for helping one's partner achieve satisfaction. A feeling of failure in that area, whether spoken or unspoken, can lead to significant couple problems.

Sex therapy is frequently very effective in treating these couple's issues, which are not due to underlying organic or medication causes. Various self-help plans also are available to educate the woman and her partner in a better understanding of their anatomy.

Masturbation is an important part of sexual intimacy. Diverse studies have shown that sex therapy can help many women to become more orgasmic through masturbation. After that, they will often become orgasmic during intercourse with a partner.

Consider the type of stimulation you need to achieve orgasm. It may differ from what you and your partner are currently practicing. Open communication and true intimacy with your partner is necessary for him or her to know what is needed for you to achieve orgasm. Sharing likes and dislikes in touching each other helps clarify individual preferences in types of stimulation, too.

In certain instances, marital therapy may need to be applied instead of sexual mechanics. Couple's therapy may be useful in resolving areas of conflict, emotional differences, and other personal issues.

◆ ◆ ◆

Again, even when the cause of sexual dysfunction is purely organic, secondary psychogenic problems *do* occur, often making matters worse.

Personal and/or psychological problems, such as depression, guilt, or a traumatic sexual experience often lead to FSD.

Relationship issues such as a power struggle, hostility, resentment, or poor communication with your partner can cause it as well.

A history of sexual abuse plays an important role in causing FSD. Sexual assault includes a spectrum of violence from rape to attempted rape or any unwanted sexual contact. This can include fondling, exposure, and verbal threats in the attempt to force sexual activity.

The incidence of rape and sexual assault according to National Surveillance Statistics is .03 percent of the female population, or about 300,000 incidents of rape and 400,000 incidents of sexual assault reported each year. Over a lifetime, 1 in 6 women will experience sexual assault or abuse.

Studies have also shown that 11 percent of sexual assaults are committed by strangers, 26 percent of the assaults are caused by a family member, 35 percent by a friend or acquaintance, and 22 percent by an intimate partner. Only 28 percent of rapes are reported to police.

Childhood sexual abuse is any forced sex on children below the legal age of consent. Such abuse can impair childhood development and adult sexual functioning and may also have long-term impact from acute physical harm such as injuries, scarring, chronic pelvic pain, sexually transmitted diseases, HIV, infertility and pregnancy. The psychological damage to the child can be equally if not more devastating.

Female sexual problems based on a history of childhood sexual abuse can cause uninformed partners to feel dysfunctional and blame themselves. If the woman who has been abused does not honestly share that history with her partner, he/she is in for a very rough and miserable time without, in some cases, ever knowing why.

If sexual aversion is your problem because you have been abused sexually including rape, this condition can be treated with the help of a sexual trauma specialist using psychological techniques such as desensitization and working through past issues.

Typically, individual therapy is implemented first in the treatment program. Once the trauma memories are resolved, sex therapy may or may not be necessary. If the patient has a history of rape, this issue may need to be addressed before couples therapy is attempted.

Sex therapy may also benefit those with severe mental health issues such as eating disorders and various manifestations of adult sexual dysfunction from teen and even adult promiscuity, post-traumatic stress disorder, heavy drug use, and alcoholism.

Sex therapy can be of great help to those suffering from the following:

- Significant/persistent depression.

- Severe marital conflicts.

- Long-term dissatisfaction with relationship.

- Substance abuse problems.

- Unresolved emotional issues.

- Prolonged sexual difficulties.

Whom should you see? The best advice is for you to go to a licensed sex therapist in your community. Be sure to ask your doctor to recommend a therapist who is certified by the American Association of Sex Educators, Counselors, and Therapists (AASECT), or who is a member of the Society for Sex Therapists and Research (SSTAR), or any other accredited society (see Appendix B).

A psychologist, psychiatrist, or social worker may be helpful in dealing with some of the above problems, but they may not be specialists in sexual dysfunction.

Specialists in sexual dysfunction will explore many areas for complete assessment in the first interview. The specialist is trained to put you and your partner at ease in talking about such personal topics as:

- Family history.

- Unresolved issues and attitudes towards sex.

- Religious upbringing and current beliefs.

- Sexual issues including puberty/early sexual experiences/masturbation.

- Body image problems.

- Eating disorders where applicable.

- Current relationship (with partner, if possible).

- Fantasies.

- Sexual encounter details, including intercourse and problems if any of arousal, desire, or orgasm.

We should mention here that availability of pornography has become a serious issue with increased use of the Internet. Web sites can be the catalyst for many addictions besides shopper's obsession or online buying such as sexually oriented chat rooms and the previously mentioned cyberporn. We should include "phone sex" as an addiction. If you and/or your partner see this as a problem, sex therapy may be the answer.

A recent MSNBC.com survey found up to 80 percent of respondents spent so much time hunting for erotica they were in danger of losing jobs or relationships. Prior to entering the world of cybersex, they had no problems of sexual addiction.

When do you know if you are a cybersex addict? MSNBC "sexploration" columnist Alvin Cooper believes if you spend 11 hours or more a week on the erotica sites and score highly on a psychologically scale of sexually compulsive behavior, you qualify as a "cybersex compulsive".

Some findings of the survey showing the differences between men and women include:

86 percent men and 14 percent women seek online sex.

49 percent women and 23 percent men prefer chat rooms.

50 percent men and 23 percent women prefer visual online erotica.

Is online sex really a bad thing? Contrary opinions, excluding those of the "adult content" industry, say that cybersex can be used in positive ways. If you are in a relationship, surfing for erotica together, the same as consensual couples watching XXX films together, may enhance your sex lives. But always remember that communication in this situation is essential.

When one of the partners secretly spends time compulsively on the Internet, whether merely as a voyeur, in chat rooms, or making dates, something is lacking in the relationship. Once aware of this compulsive behavior, the other partner should deal with the problem and if necessary seek couple therapy before irreparable damage has been done to the relationship. After learning her partner has been compulsively seeking sex on the Internet, a woman will often lose trust in their relationship.

If you or your partner think sex addiction is the issue, then classic 12-step groups are available, such as Sex and Love Addicts Anonymous.

Regardless of the problem, the therapist should help the couple define realistic goals of therapy, possible approaches, and solutions.

TWENTY-FIVE

Will It Also Work For Women?

For appropriate women with FSAD and normal androgen levels, your doctor may consider the "off-label"
use of Viagra as a possible therapy, even though it has
not yet received approval by the FDA. Positive reactions
to sildenafil therapy are increased arousal and, therefore, potentially increased desire, heightened sensations,
and satisfaction.

Pfizer recently funded a 12-week study of 577 pre-menopausal women with an average age of 37 and a wide spectrum of FSD. They were recruited from Western Europe,
Canada, and Australia. Neither the women nor the doctors knew which woman received Viagra or a placebo.

Depending upon the dosage of Viagra, 30 to 50 percent of the women said they were helped. So did 43 percent of the women who were given the placebo. The study
concluded that Viagra® seemed to be safe but the results were a statistical wash. Some doctors believe the
importance of blood flow in the female sexual response
has yet to be clearly demonstrated.

Regarding Viagra (sildenafil), the male anti-impotency
drug was used in another small study of post-menopausal

women and was proven to be generally efficacious, as early trials have shown.

Doppler ultrasound was used on women taking sildenafil and a control group using a placebo to measure clitoral blood flow following intake of the medication. Researchers found that Viagra increased blood flow to the vagina and clitoris, increased vaginal lubrication, improved ability to orgasm, and enhanced sexual satisfaction.

More FDA (Food and Drug Administration) trials are continuing. At this time, be aware that the following women should NOT take Viagra: Anyone who is on nitrates (such as nitroglycerin sublingual taken under the tongue), anyone suffering from significant heart disease; those taking multiple anti-hypertensive agents, and those of childbearing age (unless on contraceptives).

For women with depression or on SSRI medications, taking 50 mg of Viagra one hour prior to sexual activity can be effective therapy for their symptoms, but you must, however, have a prescription from your doctor.

For women who have had hysterectomies and manifest the typical symptoms of FSD, studies looking at the effect of sildenafil therapy showed significant improvement with doses of 100 mg prior to sexual activity and a decrease in many sexual complaints. However, as with men, a small percent of women may experience headache, flushing, dizziness, or nausea if they take sildenafil.

Because of side-effects resulting from oral sildenafil, doctors have been experimenting with a Viagra topical, essentially crushed pills mixed with a water-soluble cream. A New York urologist has developed what he calls a topical "Dream Cream" for women from an asthma medication (currently being tested as a male impotency drug) and L-arginine, an amino acid.

The off-label usage of topical prostaglandin E-1 (PGE-1) has been reported as beneficial in some women with symptoms of FSAD. Also, various studies are underway to evaluate the role of newer classes of phosphodiesterase inhibitor drugs in women, although it is still too early to predict how successful these agents will be for FSD.

Certainly, more studies are needed before Viagra or any other phosphodiesterase inhibitor type drug will be approved by the FDA to treat Female Sexual Dysfunction. So far, evidence supporting the use of these various medical therapies for FSD clearly suggests they are relatively safe.

TWENTY-SIX

Estrogen Replacement Therapy

Nearly all women at some time in their lives are going to be affected by lack of estrogen. Indeed, 50-million women are post-menopausal and this population is growing as the Baby Boomers age. Up to 25 percent of them may show symptoms of estrogen deficiency or vaginal atrophy at some point in their lives.

FSD among post-menopausal women is more common than people realize, but they do not have to live with the problem or consider it an inevitable part of aging. Fortunately women today are more aware of sexual problems and likely to discuss the matter with their physicians. Having had an active healthy sex life, they now know that they can continue enjoying it even after menopause.

In the past there was concern about offering oral or systemic estrogen replacement therapy to women with a family history of breast cancer or other estrogen-associated malignancies. Recent research has discovered a safe method of delivering hormone replacement. Scientific studies have looked at the effect of estrogens applied topically (directly on the body), and concluded that it is a very safe and effective treatment option for these women.

Topical estrogen enables women to better tolerate friction during sexual intercourse because it thickens the walls of her vagina, makes it more pliable, and helps increase lubrication.

A woman's personal physician will outline a therapy plan and demonstrate a technique for effective topical application of estrogen cream. How often and how long, depends upon the thinness of the tissue, but the patient can often see improvement within a few weeks. Application of the topical estrogen cream can range from once a day, to two or three times a week on alternating days. Often patients can determine their own dose as to what amount makes the symptoms disappear and continue applying it as long as they receive benefit.

Estrogen cream may be applied with an applicator. Although this is an effective way to replenish local estrogen, it can sometimes cause injuries if the tissue is especially thin. An alternative method is to use a small amount of the estrogen cream on the fingertip and apply it to the outer portion of the vagina, labia, vulva and the outer portion of the urethra as directed by her physician.

Addressing the concerns of topical estrogen usage in women, the main question is one of absorption. Since the vaginal wall is often *thin* at the start of estrogen replacement therapy, there can be some absorption by other parts of the body with systemic side-effects: mild breast tenderness, nausea, and over-sensitized nipples. But typically within a few weeks, there is a significant thickening of the vaginal lining and absorption is virtually eliminated, similar to other steroids such as hydrocortisone used for a rash.

Various formulations of estrogen can be applied topically. Many physicians prefer to use estradiol cream or Estrace™ cream by Warner Lipcott. Either can be effective in a much lower dose than conjugated estrogen. Also, they will not affect the liver and therefore have significantly higher safety levels. The Estring Ring™ (Pharmacia Upjohn) is another effective treatment option for women.

Oral estrogen therapy probably should not be used on patients with a history of breast cancer.

Up to 25 percent of women who take oral estrogen for hormone replacement may still display symptoms of estrogen insufficiency. In such cases, they may also use topical estrogen replacement therapy, as recommended by their physician.

TWENTY-SEVEN

Androgen Insufficiency Syndrome And Androgen Replacement Therapy

As stated in earlier chapters, women generally have lower levels of androgens than do men. Although the role of androgens in female sexual arousal is less understood than the medical profession would like, we do know that steroid hormones and androgens play a vital role in female sexual response. They are essential in maintaining the structure and function of the genital tissues to allow sexual arousal response in women and may also play a role in enhancing the effectiveness of new oral therapies for FSD.

Signs of androgen deficiency syndrome in women include a decrease in arousal, poor libido, decrease in orgasm, and androgen values below normal or in the "lower third" of the *normal* range. This accounts for more than *half* of women who have sexual dysfunction.

The lining of the vagina contains significant amounts of estrogen receptors. Placebo controlled studies have shown that in menopausal women, estradiol is more effective in restoring sexual function when used in conjunction with testosterone therapy. When applied topically, it leads to changes in the urethra and area around the urethra as well as its function, including improved continence, reversal of vaginal atrophy with increased thickening of the lining of the vagina, symptom relief, and restored sexual function.

Trials are currently underway to evaluate testosterone replacement with gels, patches and oral forms. Both testosterone and DHEA levels decline as women age. A recent study in Melbourne, Australia, showed an increase in sexual response in women after an oral dose of testosterone was given, suggesting that levels of testosterone are directly related to the physiology of arousal and orgasm.

However, direct testosterone replacement therapy may have certain adverse effects, especially in pre-menopausal women. Potential risks for women may involve breast cancer and damage to a fetus during pregnancy.

Other possible side-effects may include increased risk of heart attack and liver damage. These medications should only be used under the direct supervision of a qualified physician.

Also still in clinical trials is a testosterone patch for women whose hormone levels have declined. The patch is applied to the abdomen to increase libido.

In January 2001, Cellegy Pharmaceuticals initiated an expanded Phase I/II clinical trial of Tostelle®, a transdermal testosterone gel product for women who have testosterone deficiency and FSD. 18 naturally menopausal women participated in the trial and received varying doses of the product. At the end of the trial, their bioavailable levels of testosterone were similar to those in young women without significant side-effects. This study is continuing to determine the optimum dosing regimen.

At the end of 2000, a committee from the American College of Obstetricians and Gynecologists (ACOG) considered the role of androgen replacement therapy to treat women with low sex drive. The report concluded that younger women who have had their ovaries removed were most likely to benefit from the treatment. The committee also urged proper monitoring for side-effects.

Testosterone Gel and related topical agents for women with low libido are mostly in the clinical trial stage. Anecdotal studies vary from success to failure in women who had undergone hysterectomy or had ovaries removed. We have no reliable controlled studies of testosterone use on these women.

When successful, the woman experiences more sensation, improved lubrication and better arousal. If the topical gel or cream is rubbed on the clitoris, it might induce multiple orgasms.

12. Dr. Hakim's Office

Dr. Hakim looked up from Mrs. Watson's medical records and greeted her and Mr. Watson when they entered and sat opposite his desk. He had never seen them so happy.

The 52-year-old woman and her husband had come in six months ago to see if he could treat her problem. Questionnaires and exams showed that Mrs. Watson had poor desire, less than 20 percent of what it used to be, a 50 percent decrease in her ability to achieve orgasm, and low levels of various androgens. All in all, she had a multidimensional problem of sexual dysfunction and hoped Dr. Hakim could make it a win-win situation for both of them.

Mrs. Watson complained that she had no desire and sex often led to less than thrilling experiences. "It was not fulfilling when I wanted to make love."

Obviously it had affected her entire relationship with her husband whose sexual function was reportedly as good as when they met in college. Although she used to enjoy having sex, she felt she'd become merely a receptacle for his pleasure. That was why she began to focus on other activities, such as reading books. Turning away from her husband sexually was distressing enough for him, which led to further anguish for her. She wanted to make the situation better for herself and her husband.

Mrs. Watson was evaluated and shown to have androgen deficiency. She was treated with DHEA at 50 mg a day, and in three months showed significant improvement in arousal and desire, and increase in orgasm capability. They also saw a continued and significant improvement in normalization of her hormone levels at six months.

"Mrs. Watson, you've been taking 50 mg of DHEA each day for the past six months, and from both your smiles, I suspect the situation has improved beyond the results of the first three months."

"Doctor, you said give it six months, and you were right. My sexual desire has improved. I'm more rapidly aroused. And, I'm finding it easier to achieve orgasm again. I even feel a significant improvement in spontaneity, as you call it. Yes, I can honestly say that sexual activity is more pleasurable than it's been in a long time."

"In fact," Mr. Watson said, "her arousal time is so decreased that even on those occasions when she is not initially interested in sex, I can often arouse her much more quickly."

Mrs. Watson took her husband's hand. "And sex with Arthur has been so pleasurable, I've been initiating it more and more. I love this man."

"Lucky me," Mr. Watson said.

"Like you said, doctor, DHEA is truly the magic pill."

TWENTY-EIGHT

The Magic Pill

Although a number of adrenal hormones, such as cortisone and aldosterone, are constant throughout our life, DHEA and DHEA-S levels are not. They appear in abundance at birth, peak in a female around the ages of 10 to 12 (**adrenarche**), decrease over the next several years, increase again at the onset of menses, and reach constant levels until about age 50, after which we see a steady decline.

Researchers at Boston University believe that the **17-20 Lyase enzyme**, which is so important in the normal testosterone hormone pathway, can be deficient. This hormone is activated at female puberty, the time of adrenarche, and is heralded by the growth of hair under the arms.

The adrenal steroid pregnenolone is converted to DHEA by this 17-20 lyase. At some point in a woman's life this enzyme **inactivates** prematurely. This condition has been referred to as **17-20 lyase deficiency**.

Current thinking holds that the 17-20 lyase can become inactivated during a woman's life as a result of a host of causes: Nursing after childbirth, rape, stress, or infertility. When inactivated, it can lead to sexual dysfunction.

Much clinical evidence today shows that 17-20 lyase is critical to a woman's sexual response, even if she has no other signs of adrenal deficiency. Hence, she can appear perfectly healthy. You may only see sexual dysfunction and depression when her 17-20 lyase becomes inactive.

Unfortunately instead of trying to understand this syndrome, the medical community typically rushes to prescribe SSRI antidepressant drugs for these women, which often worsens the condition.

How should these women be treated? True, you can give them testosterone or testosterone with estrogen, but these treatments can cause side-effects such as facial hair and acne.

Now there is the "magic pill" for women who have Androgen Insufficiency Syndrome (AIS) with none of those side-effects, and it performs to expectations.

What is the magic pill?

DHEA!

What is DHEA?

DHEA is a human adrenal gland androgen and precursor of such steroids as androstenedione, 5-D-androstenediol, and testosterone. While testosterone is the main male hormone affecting sexual response, it is only one of several androgens that impact on a woman's sexual function.

DHEA can be obtained without a prescription. It is available at supermarkets, health food stores, airports, just about anywhere *and DHEA can change a woman's life.*

Much emerging literature on DHEA has come out, and treatment with 50-100 mg per day has been shown to be very successful in these women. In some cases higher doses of DHEA may be necessary if the body has very poor absorption.

Which DHEA should you purchase? You must be very careful as to which form of DHEA you get. The key is to find the most pure and reliable form available to guarantee adequate dosing and absorption. One of the problems, however, is that different commercial DHEA supplements that are available have various impurities and often do *not* contain the stated amount in milligrams. The careful consumer should research and look for a reputable form that the body efficiently absorbs without impurities.

A recent double blind study appeared in the New England Journal of Medicine. Women taking 50 mg of DHEA each day showed a strong increase in sexual function. Another recent study in France showed that after 6 to 12 months of using DHEA, women reported a significant increase in their sexual function. Anecdotally, many of my patients have had the same results after I have prescribed DHEA and certain other nutrients.

Hence, DHEA may be the most physiologically effective way of treating women with androgen insufficiency syndrome due to suspected inactivity of the adrenal enzyme 17-20 lyase. That is why DHEA may truly be her *magic pill.*

Remember this, if the 17-20 lyase enzyme is active, the body will manufacture DHEA naturally. If it can't, why not replace what the body cannot make? It seems like common sense.

◆ ◆ ◆

A DHEA PLAN FOR WOMEN:

After appropriate FSD evaluation by your doctor and a diagnosis of androgen insufficiency syndrome is made, the female patient should find a reliable form of DHEA. Most women will take 50 mg a day and be tested at base line, three months, and six-month intervals for levels of DHEA, testosterone, and other androgens. After re-evaluation at three months and beyond, increases in DHEA dosage may be necessary.

Typically, we see improvement in all phases of sexual response including desire, arousal, orgasm, and satisfaction, verified by new scores in the Female Sexual Function Index and Female Sexual Distress Scale.

The most commonly reported outcomes following DHEA therapy are increased spontaneity and decreased time to reach arousal. Whereas it used to take women up to 60 minutes or more to become sexually aroused with stimulation of the genitals, after DHEA therapy they find that arousal occurs more easily, more rapidly, and often with just touching or caressing, or even having thoughts about sexual activity. Yes, women often see a return of fantasies as well.

There is a common misnomer about the linear relationship of female sexual response, specifically beginning with *desire* leading to *arousal* followed by *orgasm*. What we find with their use of DHEA is that women have a significant, incredible increase in their spontaneity and arousal, so much so that arousal drives desire.

Essentially, they can say, "Wow, now I can initiate sexual activity."

Hence, the increase in desire is secondary to increase in arousal. This is similar to men experiencing increased desire after regaining their sexual function and improving their erections.

Studies in the New England Journal of Medicine show that premature cardiovascular deaths are more likely to occur amongst those with the lowest DHEA-S measurements; hence, attempts to increase and maintain vigorous DHEA levels is currently being investigated.

Recent studies of DHEA treated women have reported an increased sense of well-being and sexuality including fantasies, often within a month of the onset of DHEA therapy as compared with a placebo group, which reported no changes. Older women with lower DHEA serum levels and low adrenal functions increased their libido within 6 months of treatment, and after 12 months said they had significant improvements in masturbation and in all phases of sexual activity.

◆ ◆ ◆

Does DHEA have side-effects? Generally it does not at the recommended dosages. Occasionally, a woman might experience breast tenderness or mild acne, which are not anywhere as severe as the side-effects from clinical doses of testosterone and other androgen replacements.

Some other worries about DHEA have to do with issues of breast cancer, which appears in one of eight women in general, a horrible statistic. First the relationship between estrogens and breast cancer is well established. That is why there has been concern that DHEA may cause abnormally high levels of estrogen. A steroid that is related to sex has the potential to increase estrogens.

However, all studies to date in the United States and abroad have not seen any increase in estrogen above the *normal* range when a woman uses 50 mg of DHEA a day. We see only a **normalization** of estrogen levels, not a **super-physiological** (higher than normal) increase. Furthermore, DHEA treatment is not seen as a risk of breast cancer due to increased estrogen production.

Another major concern is the relationship between DHEA and fetal genital abnormalities or anomalies. DHEA *can cross the placenta* and, for example, the female fetus may be exposed to elevated levels of testosterone and become "virilized" with pronounced male features. So the warning is that all women who are pre-menopausal, of childbearing age without having had a hysterectomy, and have the possibility of becoming pregnant *must* use birth control if they are going to use DHEA. I cannot say this more emphatically: While breast feeding, women should *not* use DHEA.

These considerations need to be taken into account and fully discussed by a physician with the patient when prescribing treatments prior to therapy for pre menopausal women with FSD.

◆ ◆ ◆

Second line therapies can be prescribed for women taking DHEA who have normalized androgen levels but still experience problems of arousal. For instance, various nutritional or dietary supplements, as well as sildenafil/Viagra have been proven somewhat effective for some women whose androgen levels are normalized.

The EROS-Clitoral Therapy Device (CTD)® from UroMetrics™ is another treatment option for women if their androgens are normalized. EROS will be described in greater detail in a subsequent chapter. It is not a vibrator but rather a device that enhances engorgement and improves lubrication.

Long overdue, real science has been applied to female sexual dysfunction within the past couple of years. And more research needs to be done. However, it is important to note that DHEA has successfully treated women with FSD, secondary to androgen insufficiency syndrome. In fact, DHEA is capable of increasing androgen and testosterone, improving sexual function, and decreasing personal sexual distress without significant side-effects. This non-prescription *magic pill* is the latest advance in treating female sexual dysfunction.

However, as in all therapies, you should always consult with your qualified physician before beginning treatment, and *do not* exceed the 50 mg daily dose unless otherwise prescribed by your MD.

13. Dr. Hakim's Waiting Room

If Elizabeth thought she was going to have some peace and quiet while she waited for Brad, she was mistaken. Everyone in the waiting room turned to gape at a 50ish woman with a loud, raspy voice speaking on her cell phone as she came out from the doctor's office.

"Yes, it's me, Diana. Just saw the doctor. Calls my inability to achieve orgasm, anorgasmia. Yes, I told you ... vibrators don't work ..." She sat down in the waiting room. "... and it's causing me all kinds of distress. Tests show I've got low sexual desire and arousal. My Harry? Puh-leez! No more intimacy. Not that he's ever been Mr. Stud anyway. There's more. You know I came here to hear the results of my physical and all those tests I took ...

"Oh, you really want to know? My hormone, DHEA, and testosterone levels are normal, but he found that I've got high cholesterol and mild diabetes. My physical was normal, but sensory testing revealed numbness in my clitoris and vagina. And they did a special blood flow test with some sort of ultra-sound ... called Duplex Doppler or something ... sounds like a weather report ... seemed I was abnormal ...

"The treatment you ask? Honey, let me blow your mind. Ever hear of a device called EROS-CTD?"

"No? Didn't think so. Dr. Hakim's nurse showed me how it works, and Wow! He gave me a prescription for the little sucker, pun intended ...

"You can joke, honey, but that's exactly what it is. Basically, you attach it to the clitoris, turn it on and a suction mechanism generates blood flow down there."

151

Diana listened, then laughed. "You're right! If it works, who needs men!"?

"I do," Elizabeth said to herself. She looked at her watch again. Brad was now half an hour late. If he didn't keep the appointment, she had no idea what she would do next.

TWENTY-NINE

FDA Approved

EROS-CTD (Clitoral Therapy Device, Urometrics, MN) is a small hand-held battery-powered vacuum apparatus. Recently approved by the FDA, EROS-CTD enhances clitoral engorgement by increasing clitoral and vaginal blood flow, arousal, sensation, sexual response, orgasm, and satisfaction. It has been very successful in treating Female Sexual Arousal Disorder.

EROS is similar in theory to vacuum erection device therapies available to men. "A one of a kind," said Dr. Diane Mitchell, the FDA's clinical reviewer of the product.

"It is the beginning of, hopefully, a plethora of therapeutic devices and drugs that we will have available for women who suffer personal distress with these problems," said Dr. Irwin Goldstein of Boston University.

In a recent study of 25 women, 15 suffered from FSD. 7 of the 15 said the EROS device helped them to achieve orgasm more easily, 12 felt more sexually satisfied, and all experienced more sensation. Of the 10 women classified as "normal", 4 said EROS helped them to reach orgasm more easily, and 4 reported more feelings of sensation.

Tests showed that more than 60 percent of women who used EROS-CTD showed significant improvement in arousal, sensation, lubrication, ability to have orgasm, and overall sexual satisfaction.

It is safe and efficacious and has enabled physicians to offer an FDA-approved, non-pharmacological therapy to their patients for FSD treatment.

For those with FSD as a result of diabetes, EROS testing resulted in improved vaginal arterial dilation and blood flow with increased vaginal engorgement and lubrication and significant improvement in all areas of sexual function and satisfaction. EROS-CTD, which is also successful in treating disorders of lubrication and orgasm, is available only by prescription from your doctor.

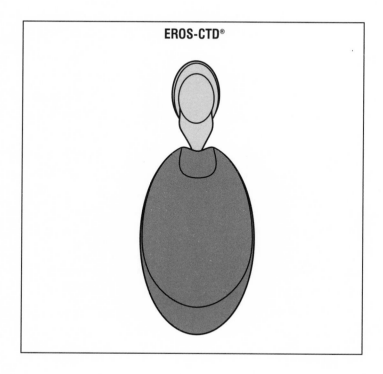

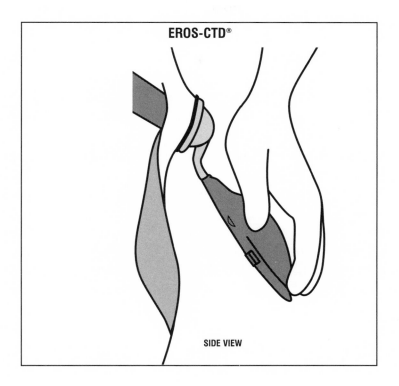

EROS-CTD®

SIDE VIEW

THIRTY

In The Future For Women

New compounds on the horizon are being evaluated both clinically and in laboratories for the possible treatment of FSD. One such treatment option to increase vaginal blood flow and increase female sexual excitement is VIP (vaso-intestinal peptide). VIP may in fact be a major neurotransmitter that is involved in the neurovascular supply to the genitalia. VIP compounds, including topicals, are currently under investigation.

Women suffering from hypoactive sexual disorder, inability to fantasize about sex, lack of interest or desire for sexual activity participated in a recent study using Buproprion. Up to 40 percent of the women who were treated with this medication over a two-week period reported improved sexual desire and sexual satisfaction. This study suggests that Buproprion may be effective for treating hyposexual disorder.

Another new therapy is apomorphine hydrochloride, a dopamine agonist or brain acting chemical that can be given sublingually (under the tongue) or nasally. Studies have shown that the drug is safe and well tolerated. It significantly improves sexual function in women measured against a placebo group. FDA based trials are ongoing.

New generations of available oral phosphodiesterase inhibitors, as well as topical agents, are currently being investigated as possible treatment options for women with FSD.

Finally, as a bridge to the next section on male erectile dysfunction, researchers have identified an enzyme, arginase, which can short-circuit a biochemical pathway critical to sexual arousal by blocking blood flow and causing sexual dysfunction in both women and men. Better yet, they also found a second molecule that can neutralize arginase. This research may lead to an effective agent for the treatment of SD in men and most women. More information about arginase will appear in the next section.

As you have read in this section on FSD, we are *only beginning* to understand the physiology of female sexual function and dysfunction. With research and studies expanding our knowledge, we will discover more preventative measures and treatments to sustain or restore sexual health for both genders.

14. Dr. Hakim's Office

Although Brad hadn't yet arrived, Elizabeth decided to begin the evaluation process herself.

Dr. Hakim looked up from Elizabeth's medical records and smiled at the young woman seated opposite him.

"Your answers to the sexual function index, and sexual distress questionnaires seem to indicate that you have no obvious sexual dysfunction. Your medical history and physical examination were normal. You know, however, that you should think about quitting smoking."

"I quit four years ago, then started up again about a couple of weeks ago. This problem with Brad ... "

"I understand the stress any form of sexual dysfunction causes, but smoking cigarettes is one of the most harmful things you can do to your body." Dr. Hakim picked up a piece of paper. "Here is a report from the Surgeon General who announced that tobacco has become the leading killer of women. Every three-and-a-half minutes a woman dies from smoking. Aside from eight types of cancer, heart disease, and other lung diseases, which affect both genders, women smokers run the risk of menstrual irregularities and earlier menopause, infertility, bone-thinning osteoporosis, arthritis, cervical cancer, and dangerous blood clots if they use birth control pills. All obviously impact on a woman's sexual function, quality of life, and self-image. Also, vanity might be a strong motivation for you to quit. Some believe that certain women who smoke also prematurely get 'smokers' face', essentially more lines than they normally would have if they

158

didn't use cigarettes … especially if they spend any time in the sun."

"I know. They're poison. I went cold turkey once. I can do it again."

"Now then, what exactly is the problem that brought you here, as you see it?"

"Lately, sex with my husband, Brad, has been pretty disappointing. He either goes soft inside me, or he gets off too quickly and just leaves me lying there unsatisfied. I have to bring myself to orgasm. I can do it by myself quite easily."

"How long have you been together?"

"A little over seven years. We met when I was a senior at college and he was finishing law school. We lived with each other for almost five years, then married two years ago after I got my Ph.D. No kids yet."

"And how many partners did you have before him?"

Elizabeth thought for a moment. "Four. No one special. And don't misunderstand. I love Brad and find him desirable. He's great at foreplay when he isn't tired. "

"What type of work do you do?"

"Marketing. I started my own PR company a little over a year ago."

"And your husband? What type of law does he practice?"

"He just changed jobs. He used to be a public defender. Six months ago he opened his own firm."

"He works long hours?"

"During the week we both get home around ten, ten-thirty. Lately on weekends too."

"Probably both exhausted?"

"Yes."

"Then, is it possible that sometimes you're forcing yourselves to have sexual intercourse?"

"Maybe."

"Did you ever consider that with his new business, and your own long hours, you both might be under stress and feel you have to make love because your partner expects it?"

"No, I never looked at it that way."

"And when the sex started becoming a problem, what did you think? How did you react?"

"I thought it was my fault at first, but then I changed my mind."

"Do you think your attitude, after the first time he failed to perform or satisfy you, escalated the problem?"

"I'm not sure, but I know that we sure argue more than ever, now."

*"Have you ever told him how you feel? You know, really **talk** to each other about your sexual desires and concerns?"*

"That's a good question. Honestly, no"

"I don't want to sound patronizing, but it's not uncommon for a couple's relationship and intimacy to suffer due to stress and other aspects of real life. Sometimes couples feel like they're growing apart or losing interest in each other, when in fact, it's just due to poor communication."

"What do you think the problem is, doctor?"

"I'll have to see him first."

*After Elizabeth left his office to wait until her husband arrived, Dr. Hakim reflected on the backlog of patients he still had to see. It was turning into one of **those** days.*

PART V

MALE ERECTILE DYSFUNCTION

THIRTY-ONE

Of International Concern

Women should read PART V with the same interest they applied to the earlier chapters on FSD to better understand their male partners.

Physicians throughout the world are well aware that male sexual dysfunction is indeed a global epidemic. In fact, experts have begun to question if the world can even afford to treat it.

A newspaper article from West Australia published in November 2000 reported a discussion that took place at the World Meeting of Impotence Research. The subject was *What Are the Costs for Treating Impotence and Who Should Pay for It?*

Some experts believe we should be allowed to grow old gracefully. Is it not reasonable to expect less erectile function as one ages? If you're in a relationship and sex doesn't matter, then why does it become an issue?

An assumption is if all men in the world eventually suffer from some form of erectile dysfunction and start using Viagra, it will overburden an already stretched health care economy with billions of dollars per year and communities will have to decide if they want to fund that.

In the real world of limited health care dollars, some fear that this may take away from other available treatments such as dialysis and transplants and other issues.

Other experts, myself included, believe that sexual function is a vitally important part of our relationships, self-images, and quality of life. Nothing occupies more of our time and lifestyle than concerns of sexual function and especially sexual *dysfunction.*

Consequently, it may not make sense to make sexual dysfunction appear less important. One should look at SD in financial terms other than national health costs. It causes divorce, depression, and other severe quality of life issues that result from it, potentially costing hundreds of millions, if not billions of dollars worldwide.

Perhaps the treatment of SD as a societal issue could be effective by looking to make savings in other areas, such as keeping couples and the family together. Also newer treatment options may also offer relief from SD less costly too.

"Sexercise" is another issue that is being talked about internationally. A study reported that men would decrease their chances of stroke or heart attack by 50 percent if they had sex at least 3 or 4 times a week. This was reported by doctors at the University of Bristol Research Center who concluded that sex is a legitimate form of exercise and as useful as other forms of aerobic activity.

In a study of 2400 men, they found that men who had sex and orgasm three or more times a week were *half* as likely to suffer stroke or heart attack. They also suggested that a minimal amount of general physical activity when combined with the aforementioned sexual activity offered significant cardiovascular protection.

THIRTY-TWO

Man's *Other* Brain

Male Erectile Dysfunction, as you will see, is often less complicated than Female Sexual Dysfunction, and I want to emphasize one important fact for men. No matter the severity of your ED problem, there is hope if not absolute certainty *that it can be cured.*

Now then, contrary to some popular belief, the following illustrations are not that of the male brain. If the labeling seems overly scientific, all you need to remember is that for the penis to function sexually, it is dependent upon good inflow and adequate storage of blood during sexual activity and normal outflow afterwards.

As is evident from the next two illustrations, the penis consists of two paired sponge-like tubes of smooth-muscle and vascular tissue (corpora cavernosa) and a separate tube (corpus spongiosum) that surrounds the urethra, the channel through which urine and ejaculation flow.

The spinal cord supplies the penile nerves, which should make it clear why spinal cord injuries can cause ED.

During erection, the penile arteries dilate and the smooth-muscle of the corpus cavernosa relaxes, causing the penis to become engorged. When this happens, the

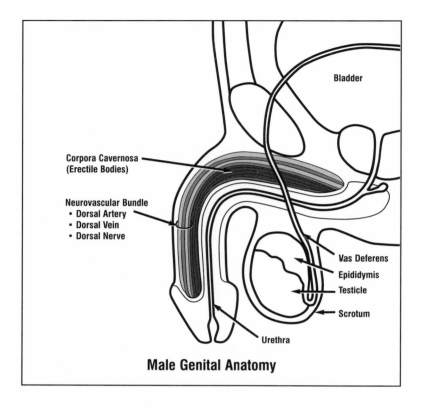

Male Genital Anatomy

veins that usually drain the corporal bodies become compressed, preventing outflow of blood and causing the penis to become rigid or *hard.*

Detumescence (flaccidity, softness) occurs following ejaculation. It is caused by a decrease in arterial blood inflow, collapse of the corporal spaces, and increased blood outflow or drainage.

To put it simply, erection occurs physically when blood surges into the penis through dilated blood vessels during sexual stimulation ("filling"). In addition

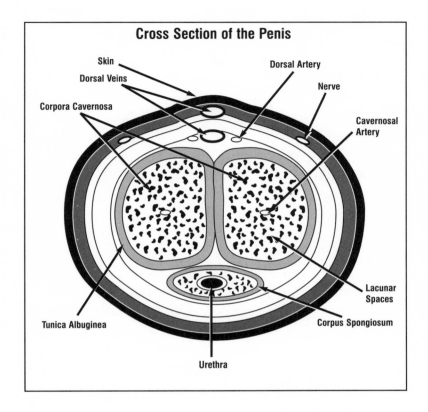

Cross Section of the Penis

to increased flow, the blood is stored or "trapped" in the penis, helping to sustain the erection ("storage"). ED or impotence occurs when blood is either prevented from filling the penis ("failure-to-fill") or there is venous leakage of the blood from the penis ("failure-to-store"), a diminished ability to sustain an erection or some combination of the two. These are the major manifestations of vasculogenic organic Erectile Dysfunction or physical impotence.

◆ ◆ ◆

Scientists may have found man's cerebral G-spot. Brain mappers who used technology from the English company *Wellcome* claim to have identified that part of the brain which becomes excited when a man is visually sexually aroused.

Dr. Redoute from the Center for Medical Research of Positron Emission Tomography (PET) in Lyon, France, found a region of the brain that is strongly linked with sexual arousal in men. Dr. Redoute and his team used PET scans to map the blood flow in the brains of nine healthy heterosexual men while they looked at photographs and short films ranging from the tame to sexually explicit.

"The aim of our study was to show the brain region directly linked with visual sexual stimulation. We found the activity of the claustrum was directly linked with the intensity of sexual arousal," says Dr. Redoute.

Other areas of the brain also reacted to the stimuli, but the activity of the claustrum was most closely associated with the level of arousal.

The claustrum is a poorly understood area in the temporal lobe of the brain. But then, the entire human brain is not well understood. Dr. Redoute's research, which is published in the journal *Human Brain Mapping*, is among the first to link it to male sexual arousal.

"It is important to know how the brain functions in healthy people to understand what happens when men have sexual problems," said Dr. Redoute.

Researchers say this knowledge of the way the brain handles the process of sexual arousal from visual images may lead to better treatments for people with sexual problems.

Currently, Stanford University has initiated study on how the brain functions in relation to sexual arousal. The multidisciplinary team includes individuals from gynecology, urology, radiology, and psychology.

Other research has shown that vitamins may also play an important role in stimulating the brain as it affects sexual function. A recent study of over 3,000 Japanese-American men living in Hawaii aged 71 to 93 years old found that combined Vitamin E and C supplements, potent anti-oxidants, reduced vascular dementia by 88 percent and was associated significantly with improved sexual function and cognitive test performance.

The two vitamins interact well together, and it was suggested that a higher level of C can improve Vitamin E levels. The study, which has been ongoing for more than 25 years, further suggested that long-term use of anti-oxidants, including Vitamins C and E, may improve cognitive and sexual function in later life.

THIRTY-THREE

What Causes ED

Although the causes of erectile dysfunction are generally similar to that of female SD, certain factors are unique to the male. Both genders know that if a man has ED it is obvious. Whereas, if a woman is experiencing FSD, her symptoms are *not* as physiologically obvious as is a limp penis.

The National Institutes of Health Consensus Panel in 1993 defined erectile dysfunction as the consistent inability to attain and maintain a penile erection to permit satisfactory intercourse. Estimates are that *ED affects over 150 million men and their partners worldwide.*

Male sexual dysfunction also includes problems of libido or desire; dysfunction of ejaculation or orgasm; **Peyronie's Disease**, which can cause abnormal curvature of the penis and ED; and **priapism**, an unwanted erection that lasts for an extended amount of time.

It should be understood that in the majority of cases, the underlying cause of erectile dysfunction is primarily one of organic or physical origin, rather than purely psychogenic. While performance anxiety and other psychogenic problems are not uncommon, they typically appear only after physical failure. In fact, studies regarding the natural history of impotence revealed that severe, untreated organic erectile dysfunction is *rarely reversible* and often progressive. Hence, *early* recognition and treatment are critical

Organic erectile dysfunction can often be attributed to vascular or blood-flow factors, neurogenic factors, various drugs or medications, endocrinologic or hormonal factors, or trauma.

Vascular erectile dysfunction due to poor blood flow ("failure to fill"), venous leakage ("failure to store"), or some combination of the two, by far accounts for the majority of patients with organic impotence.

Here is a list of additional risk factors, which will be described in greater detail:

- Hypertension.

- High cholesterol.

- Overweight and obesity.

- Smoking.

- Pelvic Surgery (RRP).

- Radiation Therapy.

- Diabetes.

- Heart disease.

- Injuries.

- Bicycle riding.

- Endocrine problems.

- Alcohol abuse.

- Peyronie's Disease.

- Drugs.

The summary chart on the next page and subsequent explanations of medical terminology should help you better understand some of the causes of male ED.

The good news, as will be explained, is that numerous advances have been made in understanding the physiologic and biochemical mechanisms controlling penile erection.

In addition, improved clinical techniques for diagnosis and successful treatment of erectile dysfunction have been developed.

Let's look at the contemporary state of knowledge about erectile dysfunction, focusing on the pathophysiology of impotence and the current diagnostic and treatment options for this common disease.

◆ ◆ ◆

One of the earliest demographic studies looking at Erectile Dysfunction began with Dr. Kinsey, a true pioneer. Back in 1948, Kinsey and his associates estimated that between 5 and 10-million American males, approximately 1 in 10 men at that time, suffered from erectile dysfunction.

CLASSIFICATION AND COMMON CAUSES OF ERECTILE DYSFUNCTION		
Category of ED	**Common Disorders**	**Pathophysiology**
Psychogenic	Performance Anxiety, relationship problems, psychological stress, depression	Loss of libido, over-inhibition, or impaired nitric oxide release
Neurogenic	Stroke or Alzheimer's disease, Spinal cord injury, Diabetic neuropathy, Radical pelvic surgery, Pelvic injury	Failure to initiate nerve impulse or interrupted neurologic transmission
Hormonal	Hypogonadism (low testosterone levels); Hyperprolactemia (elevated prolactin levels)	Loss of libido and inadequate penile smooth-muscle relaxation
Vasculogenic	Atherosclerosis Hypertension Diabetes mellitus Trauma Peyronie's Disease Smoking	Inadequate arterial flow ("failure to fill") or impaired veno-occlusion (failure to store blood in the penis)
Drug-induced	Antihypertensives Antidepressants Antiandrogens Alcohol abuse Cigarette smoking	Central suppression Decreased libido Alcoholic neuropathy Vascular insufficiency
Other systemic diseases and aging	Old age Diabetes mellitus Chronic renal failure Coronary heart disease	Mixed

In 1994, Dr. Irwin Goldstein, the father of modern sexual dysfunction research, and his associates reported in the Massachusetts Male Aging Study (MMAS) the results of the medical and psycho-social correlates of erectile dysfunction. That broad random, community-based study suggested that the prevalence of impotence from ages 40 to 70 years is now *over 52 percent among American males*: 17 percent minimal, 25 percent moderate, 10 percent severe. Other contemporary studies indicate that impotence affects *over 30-million American men,* and that number is growing every day.

Certain groups of patients have been found to have a high prevalence of erectile dysfunction. In the MMAS study cited above, aging, hypertension, heart disease, and treated diabetes were among several physiologic variables that strongly predicted impotence.

With regard to diabetic men, impotence is an age-dependent problem, which appears earlier and is accelerated in this population. Men with diabetes have more than a three times probability of having impotence than men without diabetes. Commonly, ED develops insidiously over a period of months to years among those afflicted. Patients frequently describe diminished rigidity and reduced ability to sustain an erection.

Erectile dysfunction however, is not always a *late* complication of the disease and can occur *early* in its natural history. In fact, impotence can be the *first* clinical sign of diabetes mellitus.

Neurologic and vascular issues are common complications associated with diabetes mellitus. Poor penile blood flow, decreased storage of penile blood, and/or diabetic nerve damage can be major organic causes leading to progressive erectile dysfunction in these patients.

THIRTY-FOUR

Lifestyle Issues

As a result of more leisure time, often-relaxed morals, and a cornucopia of sensory experiences, many have become jaded when it comes to sex. Essentially, with so many options and the freedom to experience everything, we can experience sexual overload. Some manifestations of erectile dysfunction may in fact be caused by societal and/or interpersonal relationship issues rather than physical or psychogenic problems.

We have come a long way in the past hundred years from the time when the female body was imprisoned in corsets, covered with layers of clothing from neck to foot, and a man could become sexually aroused by the rare exposure of a woman's "well-turned ankle". Today, very little or nothing at all is left to the imagination in cinema and TV, advertisements, and female attire that includes "dental floss" bikinis, see-through, and micro-mini-skirts.

Over the last several decades, many men have been able to experience all their fantasies, lusts, and desires repeatedly until they find themselves completely unable to react to women and even images the way they did years before.

For some, pornographic images have become *more* exciting than reality. Anecdotally, while we were doing research for this book, several women told us their male partners required the stimulation of filmed pornography or explicit magazines during intercourse with them. The media constantly reports of wives catching their husbands seeking out cyber lovers or pornography on the Internet. Regardless of media stimuli or vast experience, all this has led to much infidelity and ruined marriages.

"Gentlemen's clubs" also known as topless bars, exist in nearly every community. While this conjures images of dirty old men leching over the naturally and surgically enhanced young dancers, on a weekend dating night the majority of customers will be men in their 20s to 40s.

Some men go to these clubs for the same reason they go to sports bars, a guy's night out for beer and camaraderie, often paying little if any attention to the dancers. For others, teasing, naked lap dancing, and other stimuli soak up their 20 dollar bills and more by the minute, and for these men in most instances there is no genital resolution.

What happens after they leave is up to anyone's imagination. If the man has a partner, does the experience stimulate him to new heights as a lover, or does it make him more dissatisfied with reality and less romantic at home? This should be an area to explore for both social historians and physicians who treat ED. Despite all of the above, many marriages can be saved and infidelity avoided if the man would communicate his sexual fantasies to his partner.

Finally a comment about hygiene: Years ago, Listerine® used to advertise how well it eliminated halitosis (bad breath) with the slogan, *Even her/his best friends won't tell her/him.* Beyond bad breath, unwashed hair, and unpleasant body odor, any man or woman who is sensitive to unwashed armpit, genital, and anal smells can be rendered impotent in one breath. Male or female, if you love your partner, how do you communicate that? If you do try to communicate, how will your partner react?

15. Dr. Hakim's Examining Room

Dr. Hakim greeted Arthur Simpson, a 55 year-old male and his 30ish second wife. Arthur had a history of complete ED for 4 years. Not surprising since the risk factors included heavy smoking in the past (quit 10 years ago), coronary artery disease, and coronary bypass surgery two years ago. Although he has not had an angina attack since surgery, he keeps sublingual nitroglycerine with him at all times.

"Your PSA and testosterone levels and lab studies are normal," Dr. Hakim said. "But you have a number of significant risk factors, as we discussed."

"Dr. Hakim, we want to know what treatments are available to cure my husband's ED," Mrs. Simpson said.

"She's been very patient and caring. I'll try just about anything, but first I want to know why I have the problem."

"We can perform some simple testing before recommending therapy," Dr. Hakim said.

Arthur Simpson looked at his wife. "Dr. Hakim, once my problem is treated, is there any risk of dying in the saddle?"

"Coital coronary? Not really. For a non-diabetic, non-smoker in your age range, the risk is one in one million per year, which doubles by having sex, but for only two hours. Here are the statistics for such events as published in The American Journal of Cardiology: Health Disease and Sexual Health."

Mr. and Mrs. Simpson took the journal from Dr. Hakim and read:

Incidence of MI (coronary) in association with specific activities:

178

Upon waking	*19%*
Psychological stress	*12%*
Heavy exertion	*5%*
Anger	*2.4%*
Post sexual activity	*1.5%*

"Regular exercise reduces the risk of MI *during sex," Dr. Hakim said. "And, a number of effective treatment alternatives are available for your erection problem, depending upon the results of further testing. We'll discuss each in detail. In your case, however, I must advise you to avoid oral therapy with sildenafil ... Viagra ... because of the potential for lethal side-effects if you need nitrate therapy."*

"We did some research on our own," Arthur said, "and we want to avoid those mechanical things ... you know ... vacuum device systems and penile implants."

"Initially, nobody wants to think about mechanical devices or surgery," Dr. Hakim said. "However, it is important to understand that no single treatment option is right for everybody. We have no 'magic' pill for men. The first step is to make a diagnosis so we can understand the degree of your problem. After that I'll recommend the best options for restoring your sexual function."

THIRTY-FIVE

Vasculogenic And Neurogenic ED

In a large number of men, erectile dysfunction can be attributed to problems with the normal blood flow to the erection resulting from systemic disease. Common risk factors associated with **Vasculogenic Impotence** either due to poor blood flow ("failure to fill"), poor storage of blood ("failure to store"), or some combination of the two include atherosclerosis (arterial blockage), hypertension, high cholesterol, hyperlipidemia, cigarette smoking, diabetes mellitus, and pelvic irradiation, to name a few.

"Failure to fill" due to a site-specific or localized blockage of the penile artery can also occur in men who have sustained blunt pelvic or perineal trauma, most typically bicycling accidents.

Atherosclerotic vascular disease and erectile dysfunction are strongly related. In fact, arteriosclerosis is probably the most common organic disorder leading to impotence.

Up to 50 percent of men with clinically significant peripheral arterial disease complain of some degree of erectile dysfunction. In 80 percent of these cases, the cause of the impotence is primarily organic. Narrowing of the penile arteries decreases blood flow to the corporal bodies and contributes to erectile dysfunction.

The presence of hypertension has been demonstrated in up to 45 percent of impotent men. In men with hypertension, erectile function can be impaired by the narrowing of the penile arteries and the effects of certain medications.

Hyperlipidemia, hypercholesterolemia, or other disturbances of lipid metabolism have been found in 40 to 50 percent of men with erectile dysfunction. It has been estimated that for every 10-point rise in cholesterol above normal, there's a 32 percent increase in the risk of sexual dysfunction. Physicians and nutritionists are studying the likelihood that overweight impotent men may recover some sexual function by eating healthier, exercising, and of course losing weight. A high fat diet and poor physical condition contribute to the narrowing of the arteries supplying blood to the penis, which prevents erections.

At a recent meeting of the American Urological Association, a study of 1,981 men (ages 51 to 88) with no known history of heart disease or diabetes was presented. They were asked about their sexual functioning. 671 (34 percent) reported they experienced poor sexual performance. Those with ED were more likely to be older, have high blood pressure, and be overweight more than men who had normal sexual function. Men who had a 42-inch waist were twice as likely to have ED as men with a 32-

181

inch waist. Those who had 30 minutes of physical activity each day were 40 percent less likely to have ED than the "couch potatoes" in the study.

Although none of the men had been originally diagnosed with heart disease, the study concluded that ED in overweight men indicates potential cardiovascular troubles, which confirms other studies.

Failure of blood to store in the penis during erection (veno-occlusive dysfunction) can also lead to ED. Poor storage of blood may be associated with vascular disease seen in diabetic patients, men with curvature or Peyronie's Disease, and old age. Traumatic injury to the penis ("fracture"), often the result of intercourse injury, can also lead to poor penile blood storage, as can surgical shunts as a result of the operative correction of priapism.

Cigarette smoking is believed by many experts to be a statistically significant independent risk factor in the development of atherosclerotic arterial occlusive disease (blood blockage) within the common penile artery, and, therefore, another activity causing impotence. Five, ten, and twenty year histories of one-pack-a-day cigarette smoking exposure is associated respectively with 15 percent, 30 percent, and 70 percent incidence of blockage of the penile blood flow.

◆ ◆ ◆

A number of neurological disorders (**neuropathy**) such as Diabetes, Parkinson's disease, Alzheimer's Disease, stroke, and cerebral trauma often cause erectile dysfunction by decreasing libido or preventing the initiation of an erection. Problems with the local nerve supply to the penile blood vessels may also lead to ED. In men with spinal cord injuries, the degree of ED depends largely on the nature, location, and extent of the lesion.

The presence of accompanying bladder or bowel dysfunction (i.e. incontinence) may provide further indirect evidence of impairment of the penile nerves. Because both the bladder and penis receive their nerve supply from common origins, nerve damage to the bladder can co-exist with neuropathy of the penis. Testing of the penile nerve supply may be performed in selected cases in order to identify neurological abnormalities of erection.

To summarize, numerous advances have been made in understanding the vascular and neurologic mechanisms controlling penile erection. This knowledge has led to improved diagnostic evaluations and better therapeutic alternatives for the treatment of erectile dysfunction, which will be discussed in detail in subsequent chapters.

THIRTY-SIX

Andropause

Andropause or "manopause" is the male equivalent of female menopause. It can be said to begin around age 40, or even earlier.

ADAM is the acronym for Androgen Deficiency in Aging Men.

What are the symptoms? Not too surprising, they include a lower sex drive that can culminate in ED, aside from other health issues and less energy.

Twenty is the age when testosterone production reaches its peak in a male. Levels may begin to diminish by about age 30, with decreases in testosterone of about 1 percent per year. Other hormonal problems can occur as well.

I feel that men and women need to be aware that they may suffer from early onset of SD and hormonal problems. Why wait until the problem is severe? When you go to your physician, do not wait to be asked (the question may never be posed) but be frank about any indications of early SD.

Diseases of the prostate, including prostatitis, may also be associated with male sexual dysfunction. Therefore, good prostate health is an important goal for all men.

Homeopathic research is beginning to suggest that nutritional supplementation may be helpful in improving prostate health. For instance, male sex organs consume more zinc than any other part of the body, and some believe that zinc is lost in our current food processing systems. In fact, certain supplements containing zinc, as well as bioflavinoids (natural plant derived compounds with potent anti-oxidant effects) have been shown in clinical studies to improve prostate health. Oysters are said to be full of zinc, perhaps suggesting one reason why they have been touted as an aphrodisiac over the years.

Androgens also influence the growth and development of the male reproductive tract and secondary sexual characteristics. Although their effect on libido and sexual behavior is well-established, the effect of androgens on normal erectile function, while probably critical, remains poorly understood.

An interesting note: Loss of even both testicles may not necessarily result in the end of a man's sex drive. In some instances, the pituitary gland takes over their functions. Sir Richard Burton, not the actor, included in his unexpurgated *Arabian Nights* bawdy tales of "stoned" (castrated) eunuchs who still managed to satisfy neglected harem wives with their erect penises.

Patients with castrate levels of testosterone can often achieve erections in response to visual sexual stimulation that are comparable in quality to men with normal levels of testosterone. This suggests that the neurovascular mechanisms, which control erection, may still be functional in the presence of low levels of androgens. However, new research has suggested that testosterone is necessary for normal smooth-muscle relaxation and optimal sexual response to oral ED medications in improving sexual function in both men and women. Further studies are required to understand how abnormal androgen function results in erectile dysfunction.

◆ ◆ ◆

Although hypogonadism is the *most* common endocrine cause of erectile dysfunction, thyroid disease, adrenal disease, and various pituitary disorders such as hyperprolactinemia (elevated prolactin) may all be associated with erectile dysfunction.

Hyperprolactinemia is often associated with low circulating testosterone levels; thus implying that prolactin blocks to some degree the peripheral action of testosterone in healthy sexual function. In impotent patients with low testosterone *and* elevated prolactin levels, potency is not restored in approximately half of those treated even when their serum testosterone levels are normalized. However, other treatment options are available as will be discussed in subsequent chapters.

Erectile dysfunction may also be associated with abnormal thyroid function. However, hyperthyroidism is more commonly associated with diminished libido and less often with impotence.

THIRTY-SEVEN

Drugs And Medications

A number of medications are also associated with sexual dysfunction. Various drugs used to treat high blood pressure (hypertension), most notably the beta-blockers, have been shown to cause impotence, possibly via a decrease in corporal perfusion pressure.

Digoxin, a frequently utilized cardiac medication, can cause impotence via its effect on the corporal smooth-muscle. By causing the smooth-muscle in the penis to "contract", the ability to "fill" and "store" blood in the erection is decreased. In fact, recent studies have supported its use for the prevention of recurrent episodes of low-flow priapism!

The class of medications known as *Selective Serotonin-Reuptake Inhibitors* (SSRI) may cause decreased erectile function. In addition, the SSRI drugs can extend the time it takes for a man to ejaculate, making the culmination of the sexual act more difficult. One positive application for this "side effect" of the SSRI family of medications is that they can be used to treat the patient suffering from premature ejaculation.

Common medications associated with ED include:

- Antihypertensives

- Narcotics

- Antidepressants

- Antipsychotic agents

- Antiandrogens

- H2 blockers

- Anticholinergics

- Psychotropics

- Neuroleptic drugs

- Beta-blockers

- Cocaine

- Lipid lowering drugs

- NSAIDs (non-steroidal anti-inflammatory agents)

- Oncologic agents

- Diuretics

- Cimetidine

- Estrogens

As stated in an earlier chapter, cigarette smoking may induce vasoconstriction and penile venous leakage because of its harmful effect on the cavernous smooth-muscle and vessels, causing impotence.

Alcohol can cause central sedation, decreased libido, and transient ED — hence the term "Whiskey Dick"! In addition, the reader should not be surprised to learn that chronic alcoholism can affect the penile nerve system and cause ED.

Illegal recreational drugs including cocaine, ecstasy, heroin, and marijuana are associated with increased erectile dysfunction, possibly via a central neurological effect. Recent studies have shown that cocaine is linked to a higher incidence of priapism because of its centrally and peripherally acting effects on calcium transport and smooth-muscle relaxation. In these patients, impotence may be the culmination of repeated incidents of veno-occlusive priapism, a painful permanent erection resulting in corporal fibrosis and abnormal vascular changes, which are commonly seen in cocaine users.

16. Dr. Hakim's Waiting Room

Brad left the receptionist's desk and sat next to Elizabeth. "Sorry I'm late. Deposition took longer than I expected. How did it go?"

"He asked me a lot of questions. He wants to see you before he ventures any opinion. Will you want me in there with you?"

"Not at first. I'd rather speak to him alone."

Elizabeth and Brad were seated opposite two men in their late 30s to early 40s who were heavily involved in conversation beside an attractive woman.

"Glad to meet you, Bob ... Frances. I'm Paul ... my card ... stockbroker and bike enthusiast ... used to ride my bicycle between 50 to 100 miles a week. About a year ago I told my primary physician about a persistent numbness in my perineum and noted that the quality of my erections had diminished markedly. My doctor gave me some Viagra, which didn't work for me. Anyway, I didn't want to be drug dependent either. So I came to Dr. Hakim. When he learned that I rode on a narrow, unpadded bicycle seat, he told me how the injury to my genital area occurred. The constant pressure from riding forced the seat into my perineum, which caused blood flow blockage in my penis and genital arteries. I stopped riding, but a year later the problem hadn't gotten much better."

"What happened then?"

"Doc did a number of erectile function tests which confirmed that the problem was due to poor blood flow to the penis. The treatment he suggested was a penile revascularization procedure, sort of a bypass type surgery for my penile arteries. That was two years ago. Now I'm as good as new. Pretty wild, huh? I'm here today for a routine follow-up. What about you?"

"Well, we do a lot of fishing," Paul said, "and one day I was working on my boat. When I attempted to jump onto the dock, I

slipped, and ended up straddling the gunwale on the port bow and smashed down right onto my balls."

Brad winced as Bob said, "And we all laughed when it happened to Benny Hill."

"Tell me about it! Anyway, as you might expect, it hurt like hell down there, and the next day I saw some bruising. Then, over the next two days I had a persistent partial erection that was painless. I was then referred to Dr. Hakim by my primary care physician."

"What did he do for you?"

"Dr. Hakim performed a few simple tests including a perineal Duplex Doppler that confirmed some sort of fistula ... "

"What's that?"

"I know ... I'm sounding like a doctor ... he said I had high flow or arterial priapism. Frances was with me when I got the results, and after consultation we agreed to try a period of watchful waiting."

"How long did you wait?"

"Unfortunately after six months, it turned out to be unsatisfactory despite normal sexual function," said Frances. "He felt uncomfortable with constant partial erections."

"So I made another visit to Dr. Hakim. I underwent selective embolization ... sorry ... sounding like a med-wonk again ... which blocked the blood flow to the fistula. But a week later I still had some residual priapism. However, after we repeated the Duplex Doppler exam, Dr. Hakim reassured me that it would resolve on its own. He was right. My penile swelling and bruising was gone in 2 weeks, and by 6-8 weeks my normal erectile function had returned."

Bob gestured thumbs-up. "Then it's good news for you."

"You know it!"

"And we want to keep it that way," Frances said. "That's why we're here for our semi-annual check up."

THIRTY-EIGHT

Physical Trauma

Although more commonly reported in men over 40, erectile dysfunction can occur in men of all ages. It is true that systemic vascular diseases, such as those due to hypertension, atherosclerosis, diabetes, or hypercholesterolemia, are more often risk factors in older men. Yet, vascular insufficiency due to genital or perineal trauma can often be associated with erectile dysfunction in young men.

Any type of blunt traumatic injury, which affects the penile blood vessels, corpora, or neurological supply, can lead to abnormal blood flow to the penis and diminished nerve supply.

Upright bicycle riding and the blunt trauma due to constant perineal pressure from a narrow poorly structured and unpadded bicycle seat, top tube, or crossbar, have been implicated as the underlying causes of erectile dysfunction in many men who enjoy this activity. Each year, thousands of men will lose the ability to achieve or sustain satisfactory erections because of genital damage caused by a narrow unpadded anatomically unfriendly saddle (seat) or sudden violent contact with the top tube or cross bar. Dr. Goldstein reported in the *Journal of Urology* that if a 150 pound cyclist falls onto the bicycle's crossbar, the force felt by his genitals would be the equivalent of a quarter ton (500 pounds).

In June, 2001, a study from Germany presented at the annual American Urological Association meeting in California also found that cycling in an upright position (with perineal pressure) versus a "reclining" position leads to poor penile blood flow and significant erectile dysfunction.

Sports injuries to the genitalia and scrotum, such as kicks or hits, that occur in football, hockey, lacrosse, and other contact sports, are often found to be the culprit afflicting these young, otherwise healthy men after complete vascular testing has been performed.

Trauma to the male genitalia may also come from sexual intercourse or sex play, and cause a penile fracture or "Broken Penis Syndrome," a form of Peyronie's Disease, which will be thoroughly discussed in a separate chapter. Once dysfunction caused by trauma is revealed by patient history, a number of specialized vascular tests can help to make an accurate diagnosis. In selected cases of traumatic arterial obstruction, microscopic reconstructive vascular surgical techniques may be utilized to help restore normal erectile dysfunction.

THIRTY-NINE

Aging, Other Systemic Diseases, And Prostate Cancer

Not surprising, sexual function can progressively decline in otherwise healthy aging men. The latent period between sexual stimulation and erection increases. Erections may become less firm. Ejaculation may become delayed, less forceful and its volume decreases. The period between erections lengthens.

Unfortunately, gentlemen, there is more to look forward to. As you age, you face a decrease in penile sensitivity to tactile stimulation, and a decrease in the serum testosterone concentrations.

About 50 percent of men afflicted with diabetes mellitus have erectile dysfunction.

Chronic renal failure has been associated with diminished erectile function, impaired libido, and infertility.

Men with angina, myocardial infraction, or heart failure may have ED due to anxiety, depression, in addition to poor penile blood flow.

◆ ◆ ◆

As the population continues to age, many men will eventually face a diagnosis of prostate cancer. Fortunately, with the advent of PSA screening and early detection, doctors are now able to cure the majority of men with prostate cancer while the disease is still localized. In fact, more than 100,000 prostate surgeries are performed in the United States each year. Once that treatment is over, it is only natural for a man to want to return to a normal sex life, and now he may have that desire fulfilled.

For thousands of prostate cancer survivors, surgical removal of the prostate (prostatectomy), radiation therapy (external beam or seed brachy-therapy), or cystoprostatectomy for bladder cancer may have some side-effects in previously potent men that will delay the patient's complete physical and emotional recovery.

The microscopic nerves and important blood vessels that stimulate erections run alongside the prostate on their way to the penis. Sometimes with radiation therapy or during a prostatectomy, these nerves or vessels are damaged in an effort to remove completely all of the cancer from the patient's body. If this happens, erectile dysfunction or the inability to achieve or maintain a satisfactory erection for intercourse may result.

Despite a "nerve-sparing" approach by the surgeon or radiation therapy, many men, especially those over 60, will experience some decrease in their potency. This loss of function is most likely a result of a combination of neurogenic and vasculogenic factors. Fortunately, excellent treatment alternatives are available to these men to help restore them to a level of good sexual function.

During the first 3 to 12 months after prostate surgery, between 30 and 70 percent of men will not be able to achieve a spontaneous normal erection. Although sexual function *may* gradually return in time, your urologist can offer several choices to improve ED and quality of life, including medical therapies and ultimately surgical implantation of a penile prosthesis (to be explained in detail in a subsequent chapter).

After either radiation therapy or surgical treatment of prostate cancer, the absence of nocturnal and sexual erections will eventually result in poor blood flow and poor oxygenation of the erectile bodies. This leads to penile corporal fibrosis, penile shortening, and permanent ED. Remember, the sooner you can restore penile blood flow, the better the chance you have of restoring sexual function and improving quality of life.

Recent testing of a new surgical procedure may offer hope to men who have had operations to remove their cancerous prostate glands. The idea is to essentially "rewire" the penis so that these men may achieve erections and have sex after prostate surgery. Nerve sparing prostate surgery can preserve the two nerve bundles that carry signals to the penis and cause it to fill with blood for erection. However, if the cancer is too close to the nerves, one or both must be severed, which often leaves the patient impotent.

The experimental surgical process removes nerves from the patient's ankle to fill in the gap between the severed ends. Although doctors concede the grafts are not as good as the original nerves, Dr. Peter Scardino, a pioneer of the process, has estimated perhaps one third of the men who have prostate surgery might benefit from sural (calf or leg) nerve grafts if the technique proves out in further testing.

What about continence? The sphincter is a muscle that contracts around the urethra to hold urine in the bladder or relaxes to let it flow out. It may be damaged during prostate surgery or following radiation therapy, which could result in involuntary loss of bladder control or urinary incontinence. After a prostatectomy, more than 40 percent of men *may* be incontinent for up to several weeks after surgery. For obvious reasons, that condition can be extremely embarrassing and an inhibitor of sexual function.

Although normal bladder control gradually returns for most men, some patients will continue to leak small amounts of urine when they cough, sneeze, or laugh. For others, the result is more severe and long lasting. In fact, a recent study showed that 5-10 percent of men undergoing prostatectomies were incontinent for at least 18 months following the procedure. While exercises, behavior modification techniques, and medications can be used to treat the majority of patients with urinary incontinence, several surgical procedures may be applied when those treatments are ineffective or inappropriate after 6 to 12 months.

Injecting a bulking material at the neck of the bladder may help replace sphincter function. While less invasive, bulking injection therapy is not always successful over the long term, and patients often need repeat procedures.

Placement of a surgical sling has been recently reported as a treatment for men with mild to moderate urinary incontinence and who have not responded to medications, although long-term data are lacking.

An effective alternative is the implantation of an artificial urinary sphincter prosthesis. The AMS Sphincter AUS-800™ (American Medical System, Minnetonka, Minnesota) urinary prosthesis has been used successfully for over 25 years. It is a small device implanted entirely within the body. The device is designed to mimic natural sphincter function, which enables the patient to control bladder storage and emptying. Long-term studies show that 80 percent of men implanted with this device were socially continent (when out in public) for over 7 years, and 90 percent of men were highly satisfied with their AMS Sphincter AUS-800 urinary prosthesis.

The key points to remember about post-prostatectomy sexual function are:

1. Curing the cancer is the most important factor. Side-effects can successfully be treated, but only if you're alive!

2. Be assured that you can have a functioning sex life after prostate cancer.

3. Although a full recovery may take some time, help is available that successfully treats the side-effects of a radical prostatectomy and for radiation therapy.

4. Impotence and incontinence are no longer inevitable for men after prostate surgery or radiation therapy.

To repeat, the first step is to contact your urologist as soon as the problems begin. Also, the organizations listed in the Appendix B provide support and information to men and their families who are experiencing these difficulties.

FORTY

More Than "Just Cough And Turn Your Head!"

As with FSD in women, the approach to curing male ED is threefold: Identification, Education, and Modification leading to Intervention.

Identification typically includes medical, sexual, and psychosocial histories by your doctor. Sexual history would include a description of current and past erectile function, orgasm, ejaculation, sensation, libido, arousal, and partner's sexual function as well. Remember, though, the first step is up to you.

Medical history includes identifying various risk factors such as diabetes, hypertension, heart disease or medications. Psychosocial history would include any experience of sexual trauma, depression, problems of self-esteem, and past or present partner relationships.

The results of the initial evaluation may be further corroborated by a variety of diagnostic examinations such as neurological, psychological, hormonal, and vascular testing.

So that you are not kept in the dark, what follows is what you can expect from a qualified urologist.

Your doctor will need your medical records as well as your willingness to honestly answer a questionnaire relating to your medical, sexual, and psychological history. Then you will undergo a comprehensive physical examination followed by specific laboratory tests.

◆ ◆ ◆

The physical examination includes evaluation of the penis during its flaccid state. Of note, the penis should be able to stretch over an inch and a half on average in length due to its normal elasticity when flaccid. Of note, the average length of flaccid penis is 3.7" and average erect state is 5.5". If stretching is less than normal, then there may be presence of Peyronie's Disease. Your doctor will look for abnormal penile curvature or "plaques" associated with Peyronie's Disease. The doctor will also perform a prostate check and evaluate testicular size and feel.

The physical also includes looking for aneurysm. The neurologic exam, such as straight leg raising, also looks for lumbo-sacral disc dysfunction. Of note, a herniated disc can cause neurogenic ED.

Next, you will undergo an endocrinologic and laboratory evaluation, vascular evaluation, and in selected patients, a neurological evaluation. Remember, ED is often the first sign of another underlying disease process.

Laboratory evaluation may include:

1. Routine hematology and chemistry profile.

2. PSA.

3. HgA1C or glucose level.

4. Lipid/cholesterol profile.

5. Hormonal profile (including Testosterone, LH, FSH).

6. Rule out Hyperprolactinemia (serum Prolactin level).

7. Rule out thyroid disease, other pituitary disorders, and adrenal disease.

Vascular evaluation (*in selected cases)

1. Penile blood flow study.

2. Penile Duplex Doppler Ultrasonography.

3. Dynamic Infusion Cavernosometry and Cavernosography (DICC)*.

4. Selective Internal Pudendal Arteriography*.

5. Cavernosal tissue biopsy*.

Neurological evaluation (in selected cases)

1. Biothesiometry (Vibration perception sensitivity testing).

2. Nocturnal penile tumescence testing.

3. Single breath beat-to-beat variation (autonomic parasympathetic neuropathy).

4. Single potential analysis: Cavernous electrical activity (peripheral nerve damage).

5. Dorsal nerve somatosensory evoked potentials.

6. Sacral latency testing.

Testing for erectile dysfunction also includes assessing axial-rigidity or buckling pressures in the erect state. This is a useful measurement of the ability to sustain an erection strong enough to penetrate a vagina. Based on Euler's formula, it takes one kilogram (2.2 lbs.) of force (axial-rigidity) for a penis to penetrate a vagina.

By using more sophisticated evaluations, a primary organic cause of erectile dysfunction is often found. However, you should remember that either a primary or secondary psychogenic problem might contribute to the sexual dysfunction. In order to maximize patient success, both the organic and psychogenic factors should be addressed. With this in mind, even if your erectile dysfunction is shown to be primarily due to an organic problem, your doctor may recommend a psychological or sex therapist's evaluation.

Always remember, impotence is a *"Couple's Disease."*

Although a physician may have to deal primarily with the patient regarding his sexual dysfunction, his partner is a vital part of the equation. Efforts to include the partner in all aspects of the diagnostic evaluation and treatment decision process are often essential to obtaining a successful outcome.

◆ ◆ ◆

Once a diagnosis has been made, your physician will discuss suggested treatments for your ED. They will depend on the causes and severity of the problem.

Regarding *education* and modification, lifestyle changes of various risk factors such as smoking are critical. Cigarette smoking can damage the lining of the blood vessels causing ED. Remember, small **ed** (endothelial dysfunction) causes large ED (erectile dysfunction).

◆ ◆ ◆

Various therapeutic alternatives are available for patients with organic erectile dysfunction including ED caused by penile arterial insufficiency ("failure to fill") and/or veno-occlusive problems ("failure to store"). These may include non-operative treatments such as lifestyle changes, behavioral psychotherapy, and vacuum erection devices. Pharmacological treatments include oral, topical, and intraurethral medications and penile self-injection therapy. Each of these options, including operative therapy, will be discussed in detail in the next few chapters.

The chapter for women on sex therapy is equally valid for men and need not be repeated here. As with women, psychosexual therapy may be necessary and should be combined with other treatments as well. Advantages are that it is non-invasive, involves a partner, and is likely to be curative. In selected cases, disadvantages are that for some it can be time consuming, the patient may be resistant, and often, physical problems are the underlying cause of the ED.

17. Dr. Hakim's Examining Room

Elizabeth and Brad watched another patient leave for Dr. Hakim's examining room. "Guess, we'll be last because I was late," he said.

Dr. Hakim greeted William, a 56-year-old executive, in a stable marriage of 30 years, with a 12 month history of Erectile Dysfunction, with poor morning erections as well.

"Doctor, since I was last here for my physical and lab tests, my erections are worse and I seem to be more tired. I wonder if my wife has lost interest in sex too, or she's worried I can't perform."

"The good news is that you have no significant heart disease, hypertension, coronary artery disease or diabetes. You're not taking any nitrate medications, and your examination was normal. Your PSA was only 1.2 and your total testosterone was 658, normal. However, your cholesterol was a little too high at 285."

"Then can you give me a prescription for Viagra?"

"Sure, not a problem. In fact, I think that Viagra is an excellent first line therapy for you. To begin, I want you to start with a dosage of 50 mg an hour before sex, but remember, it will not work as well or at all if you drink too much alcohol or eat a heavy meal before sex. Remember, too, that it requires sexual stimulation to be effective. Also, you should lower your cholesterol and start a reasonable exercise program, and for that I'm referring you to your internist."

"Okay, sounds like a plan."

"You also told me your wife has had less interest in sex lately?"
William sighed. "Yes, that's true."
"Then, I'd like to evaluate your wife in my office, or she can go to her physician if she prefers. Sexual Dysfunction is really a couple's disease, and statistically she is of an age where some form of FSD may well be impacting on her sex life too."

FORTY-ONE

Oral Non-Hormonal Treatment Of ED

New oral medications allow for improved erectile function simply by taking a pill prior to sexual intercourse. A number of non-hormonal oral medications are now available or being investigated. These medications have been effective in 40 to 70 percent of patients tested. They include Type-5 specific phosphodiesterase inhibitors (sildenafil, Viagra); Alpha-2 adrenergic blocking agents (yohimbine hydrochloride); phentolamine; and centrally acting drugs such as apomorphine.

Oral sildenafil, aka Viagra, should be taken approximately 1 hour before sexual activity and requires sexual stimulation to work. Viagra's main advantage is that it is easy to take, safe if prescribed properly, and is effective in many men regardless of the cause of their ED. Currently it costs about $10 per dose, which may run up to $300 for a month's supply. Doses available are 25mg, 50mg, and 100mg.

Viagra's beneficial effect can last up to 8 hours or more, and many men still notice it works for them the morning after as well. Be warned, however, it is less effective when taken in conjunction with alcohol or after eating a heavy meal, possibly due to poor absorption.

Studies reveal that Viagra is up to 80 percent efficacious in men with psychogenic ED.

In some spinal cord injured men, 40 to 70 percent will have success with Viagra depending upon the degree of injury. High success is noted amongst men with incomplete spinal cord lesions.

For diabetic men, the success rate of Viagra is 40 to 60 percent. However, amongst men who have undergone radical prostatectomies for prostate cancer, even with nerve-sparing procedures the success rate may be less.

Viagra is not a utopian solution for all men and has certain disadvantages. It can have side-effects of headache, dyspepsia (stomach upset), nasal congestion, facial flushing, dizziness, and "blue vision" for certain men (pilots beware); men with cardiovascular disease may also suffer. It takes about an hour to work, so lack of sexual spontaneity can be an inhibitor, and requires sexual stimulation to be effective. As a number of patients have stated, they do not always know an hour before having sex that they will be having sex. Finally, it is contraindicated with nitrate medication.

In a recent study of men using Viagra, side-effects were as follows:

- 16 percent had headaches.

- 11 percent experienced flushing.

- 7 percent had dyspepsia (stomach upset).

- 4 percent had nasal congestion.

- 3 percent experienced transient visual disturbance, commonly known as "blue haze".

Yohimbine is produced from the bark of yohimbe trees. It presumably acts at the adrenergic receptors in brain centers associated with libido and penile erection. An evaluation of 7 placebo-controlled studies of 419 men with ED from various causes found that yohimbine was better than placebo (placebo effect) for all types of ED.

Unfortunately, frequently reported side-effects of yohimbine are palpitations, fine tremor, elevation of blood pressure, and anxiety. Those who have cardiac diseases should use caution. Yohimbine is not recommended for men with severe organic ED because its benefits are marginal in such cases.

Oral phentolamine has been reported to improve erectile dysfunction. In a clinical trial of 459 men with mild-to-moderate ED, improved erections occurred in 37 percent of men treated with 40 mg of phentolamine, 45 percent of those treated with 80 mg, and 16 percent of those given placebo.

Side-effects of phentolamine can include headache, facial flushing, and nasal congestion. The FDA has not yet approved oral phentolamine, although it is currently undergoing investigation.

Apomorphine when injected or taken subcutaneously can cause erections in humans, but side-effects, especially nausea, have limited its clinical usefulness. Uprima (TAP Pharmaceuticals), a sublingual (under the tongue) formulation of apomorphine hydrochloride is currently undergoing clinical trials. Thousands of men were given the experimental drug, which, some believe, will eventually rival sales of Viagra.

Uprima acts "centrally" by increasing levels of a brain chemical that may play an important role in causing erections, unlike Viagra, which acts "peripherally" at a local level by increasing the flow of blood to the penis. Placed under the tongue prior to intercourse, the drug dissolves, and patients responded with erections within 20 minutes on average.

Unfortunately, in addition to a mixed erectile response, a number of the men tested in the United States with apomorphine suffered low blood pressure or fainted. The FDA reversed its initial conditional approval of the impotence drug and advised the company that further tests were needed.

In Europe, and possibly the rest of the world, the Uprima story continues. About 30 million European men and more than 100 million men worldwide are estimated to have ED, excluding the United States. Early clinical trials in Europe reported only mild dizziness, nausea, and headache in a small number of men taking the recommended 2 mg to 3 mg does of Uprima. In 2001 the European Union's Committee for Proprietary Medical Products (CPMP) adopted a positive attitude for Uprima.

Better news for Americans is coming from several drug companies. Palatin Technologies reported in 2001 positive Phase I results for its nasally inhaled impotence drug, PT-141. PT-141 is a peptide analog of (alpha)-MSH [alpha]-melanocyte-stimulating hormone, which stimulates the receptors that influence a variety of behaviors including sexual arousal.

In a double-blind placebo-based study of 56 healthy male volunteers, the nasally inhaled agent began to take initial effect within 5 minutes and reached maximum levels in the blood at 30 minutes with a high number of erections. Importantly, the study reported no significant changes in blood pressure, heart, or respiratory rates. Also, not one of the volunteers experienced nausea, vomiting, or fainting. PT-141 was tolerated at all doses, although a maximum dose has yet to be identified. Palatin will follow up with a Phase II trial to substantiate the Phase I results.

Eli Lilly & Co. is in a joint venture with the Icos Corporation, a biotechnology company partially owned by Bill Gates of Microsoft. They recently completed a controlled phase III trial of almost 200 men suffering from mild to severe erectile dysfunction with the oral medication IC351 (*Cialis*)®, discovered by Icos, which the company announced was effective in treating ED by inhibiting the enzyme phosphodiesterase-5.

The data was presented at the 96th Annual meeting of the American Urological Society in Anaheim, California. In this trial, the men were free without restrictions to eat, drink alcohol, and to have sex with their partners at any time after taking a prescribed dose. Depending upon their taking a 10-mg or 20-mg dose of IC351, the success rate for intercourse ranged from 70 to 78 percent, and 92 percent reported improved erections. Negative effects in this study were reported as mild to moderate, and the incidence diminished as the treatment continued. Backaches, muscle aches, and upset stomachs were the most common side-effects. The company claimed that there were no clinically significant changes in blood pressure, heart rate, electrocardiograms, and lab tests that they could attribute to IC351. Also, the drug appeared to work for 24 hours compared to a few hours with Viagra. Further trials are ongoing.

Bayer has Phase III tested **vardenafil** (another phosphodiesterase inhibitor drug) in men who have mild-to-severe ED in a controlled study with doses of 5, 10, and 20 mg. The results of this and other studies showed improvement in erections from baseline. Bayer is also testing vardenafil on diabetic patients, which, so far, shows impressive results. Bayer is in the process of submitting a new application for the drug to the US Food and Drug Administration.

◆ ◆ ◆

In May 2001, a report in the *American Journal of Medical Sciences* described how the angiotensin II receptor antagonist **Losartan®** (blood pressure medication) appeared to improve sexual function among hypertensive men. Dr. Carlos M. Ferraro of the Wake Forest School of Medicine asserted, "… our data points out that although we have always blamed medications — particularly ß-blockers and diuretics — as the cause of impotence, it is the disease process itself, probably resulting from reduced vascular compliance."

Dr. Ferraro's test treated 82 hypertensive men who had ED and 82 hypertensive men who had normal sexual function. They were given 12 weeks of Losartan therapy at 50 mg/day.

Amongst the men receiving Losartan, overall sexual satisfaction by the end of 12 weeks rose from 7.3 percent before the therapy to 58.5 percent. The number of patients who reported having sexual activity at least once a week increased from 40.5 percent to 62.3 percent. Only 11.8 percent of patients receiving Losartan reported no improvement in sexual activity. Future studies are anticipated.

18. Dr. Hakim's Waiting Room

"You're pretty young to be here, Brad" Zach said. "What is it, injury, performance anxiety?

"Probably nothing at all, or nothing serious."

"Well, young man, I'm 55, and let me tell you, it's good to be able to talk about these things. I've had a gradual onset of Erectile Dysfunction and decreased libido over the past three years. At the same time, I was experiencing job stress, nightly fatigue, and decreased frequency of intercourse. My morning erections became less frequent and sexual erections less firm. All of that quite naturally led to increased anxiety and worsening of symptoms. Performance anxiety if you will. Doc said my past medical and surgical histories were unremarkable, although I was mildly obese. Lost a few pounds since my first consultation. Never used medications, drugs, or tobacco. My social drinking is minimal. Various lab tests including those for cholesterol and prostate were normal, but my testosterone level was very low!"

"They must really give you the works here," Brad said.

"And that's a good thing too. After Dr. Hakim explained the available diagnostic and therapeutic options, and a careful explanation of the risks and benefits of each, I decided to begin testosterone replacement therapy with testosterone shots every two weeks."

"Has it worked?"

"Overall pretty well. I've experienced a marked improvement in libido, energy, and erectile function. But, I've also experienced up and down mood swings from the medication, and I find visits to the doctor every other week to be inconvenient."

"What do you think he'll suggest?"

"We've already talked about it, and he suggested switching either to a testosterone patch or gel, something called Androgel®, and apply it each day. I've been assured it'll eliminate the mood swings and at the same time it'll continue to improve my libido, energy, and erectile function."

"Does it have any side-effects?"

"Very minimal."

Brad turned to Elizabeth. "Does everyone here advertise about their problems?"

"Dr. Hakim told me that if you can't speak about it, you won't try to fix it."

FORTY-TWO

Hormone Replacement Therapy

Hormone replacement therapy, specifically *testosterone* replacement therapy should be used in the treatment of erectile dysfunction only in the presence of hypogonadal disorders or low testosterone, not as "empirical" or experimental therapy.

Historically, androgens were touted as enhancing male function. Yet, clinical studies have shown that men who have *normal* testosterone levels do *not* have improved sexual function with androgen therapy. Other disadvantages are that it stimulates growth of the prostate, and misuse can make the problem worse, specifically increased mental desire with no erections.

Patients with ED and low testosterone may be given testosterone replacement through intramuscular injection, by wearing a transdermal testosterone patch, or applying a topical gel. In these cases, testosterone replacement is employed to maintain normal serum levels of testosterone in an attempt to restore potency and libido.

In men who have low testosterone levels, oral testosterone preparations are less effective than intramuscular and transdermal preparations due to poor, inconsistent absorption. They also have the potential to cause liver problems.

Disadvantages of testosterone shots are that there is high activity after the first week ('peak') with noticeable decrease thereafter (also known as 'the trough').

Transdermal applications of the hormone can cause skin irritation and on occasion contact dermatitis.

Warning! Indiscriminate use of testosterone by men *without* hypogonadism should be avoided due to the risk of hepatotoxicity (liver damage) and diseases of the prostate.

In fact, before beginning testosterone replacement therapy in *any* man over 50, serum prostate specific antigen (PSA) levels, a digital rectal examination, and possibly transrectal ultrasound studies should be performed.

For Hyperprolactinemia (an abnormally elevated level of prolactin), MRI may reveal the presence of a pituitary tumor (aka microademona or macroadenoma). The patient may be treated successfully with medical therapy, such as Bromocriptine®. In some cases, surgical removal of the tumor is recommended.

FORTY-THREE

Vacuum Erection Devices

Some men either cannot tolerate medical therapy or the treatment fails. Not to worry — other non-invasive alternatives can be considered.

Medically approved vacuum erection devices (VEDs) and constriction rings currently cost approximately $150-450/unit. They offer a relatively inexpensive treatment and are simple to use. VEDs are non-invasive, safe in most cases with resulting penile engorgement, and have no systemic side-effects.

Another use of the vacuum erection device is as an "exercise" for impotent men who have undergone prostate or other penile surgery. It is felt that the VED can improve blood flow to the erectile bodies, and that it may also prevent or restore damaged fibrotic changes due to poor penile blood flow, low oxygen levels, and absent nocturnal erections.

Vacuum erection devices have cetain disadvantages. They can be cumbersome and may cause a less natural or *wobbly* erection, and discomfort and pain resulting from bruising or penile swelling. Hematomas, bruising, and penile numbness can occur, and the constricting ring can prevent ejaculation. Remember, the constricting ring should be used for only 20 to 30 minutes at a time. Use of VEDs does not allow for entirely spontaneous sex.

Non-medical vacuum erection devices have been widely advertised in magazines and on the Internet for the purposes of improving erection, penile lengthening, and auto stimulation. Misuse of such non-pressure regulated devices has led in some cases to penile injury and the onset of new vascular impotence.

As a cautionary example, a 46-year-old sexually active and potent man used a NON-MEDICAL vacuum pump as an outlet for self-stimulation on his already rigid penis. It worked so well for him that he kept pumping it up and creating additional vacuum. Then he heard a "pop". He actually blew out his corpora! In fact, a published analysis of the case revealed that the high pressure he generated was equivalent to having a 19-inch television set tethered to his penis and then dropped from his erect shaft. The injury and corporal scarring caused severe ED and persistent penile curvature. *Let the buyer beware!*

FORTY-FOUR

Self-injection Therapy

Another form of minimally invasive therapy includes intracavernosal or penile injections directly into the side of the phallus at its base. Various vasoactive agents currently in use include: Caverject® and EDEX® (FDA-approved alprostadil or PGE), as well as non-FDA approved chemicals. Intracavernous drug injection mixtures contain certain combinations of medications, including papaverine, phentolamine, and/or alprostadil (Trimix™). Advantages are that the injections are up to 90 percent effective with minimal systemic side-effects.

Disadvantages are that they require penile injections prior to each sex act and can cause priapism (a painful, prolonged erection). Nodules, scarring and fibrosis, and penile pain may also occur. Also, many men feel that sticking a needle in their penis every time they expect to have sex is not fun, nor is it particularly spontaneous and romantic. Understandably, patients using this treatment have a high dropout rate.

Other medications have also been studied. Vasoactive Intestinal Polypeptide is a potent smooth-muscle relaxant originally isolated from the small intestine. Its injection alone does not cause a rigid erection. When combined with phentolamine, approximately two-thirds of the men tested experienced erections sufficient for sexual intercourse. Common side-effects included temporary facial flushing (53 percent), bruising (20 percent), pain at the injection site (11 percent), and truncal flushing (9 percent). This combination is available in several European countries, but not in the United States.

Before beginning their injections at home, men must undergo appropriate training and education. The goal of this treatment is to achieve an erection that is adequate for intercourse lasting up to one hour.

As stated earlier, the two major side-effects of intracavernous injections are priapism and fibrosis or nodules. Priapism can usually be prevented through careful dosing and monitoring.

Nodules are usually caused by not following instructions and can lead to penile curvature. To prevent nodules, we routinely advise men to compress the injection site for up to five minutes, 10 minutes for men taking an anticoagulant drug.

Intracavernous injection therapy is contraindicated in men with sickle cell anemia, who are prone to priapism, those with schizophrenia or other severe psychiatric disorders, or those with severe venous leakage.

Although the response rate is high, in long-term studies 38 to 80 percent of men ceased or dropped-out of therapy within 18 months. Some patients alternate injection therapy with oral sildenafil and transurethral alprostadil, injecting themselves only when an erection of longer duration is desired.

Vasoactive agents can also be delivered intraurethrally (MUSE) by inserting a small pellet into the urethra

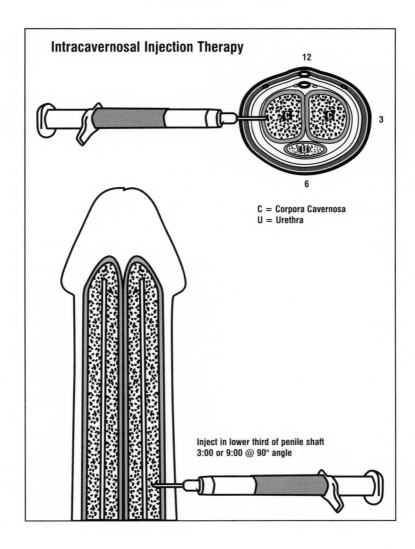

Intracavernosal Injection Therapy

C = Corpora Cavernosa
U = Urethra

Inject in lower third of penile shaft
3:00 or 9:00 @ 90° angle

through the meatus or head of the penis. The goal is for the patient to achieve a rigid erection for 30 to 60 minutes for satisfactory intercourse. These treatments may be successful in cases of psychogenic and minimal to moderate organic ED.

Transurethral alprostadil (MUSE) is a local therapy and relatively simple to use with few systemic side-effects. Unfortunately, it is only minimally to moderately effective, which is somewhat improved with Actis®, an adjustable penile-constriction device. MUSE requires office training and can cause episodes of low blood pressure and severe penile pain or aching in some patients.

As yet, the FDA has approved no transdermal medication for ED, and none is available for clinical use. Two topicals are already in Phase III testing, Topiglan®/Machro-Chem, a prostaglandin gel, and Alprox-TD®/NexMed™, a cream. It is applied to the glans of the penis prior to sexual activity where it is absorbed and induces an erection.

Nitroglycerine cream or paste and a cream containing aminophylline and isosorbide dinitrate have been used in pilot studies of men with ED. So far the results have been inconclusive.

19. Dr. Hakim's Waiting Room

Elizabeth and Brad watched a dapper gentleman enter and hand the receptionist a box of candy. "For you bella." Then he went over to one of the other patients in the waiting room. "Rocco, you had the operation yet?"

"Next week, Sal."

"Piece of cake." He looked over at Brad. "Young guy like you, you think you have it made? There ain't nothing better than a penile prosthesis."

"What's that, a fake penis?" Brad asked.

"Nah, kid, they're not dildos."

"I'm curious," Elizabeth said." What is it?"

Sal came over and sat next to her. "I'm 63 ... had high blood pressure and diabetes ... couldn't get it up. And me, a Sicilian, with the most beautiful wife in the world. Tried everything until Dr. Hakim suggested I have the inflatable implant."

"Sounds like major surgery," Brad said.

"Outpatient ... may have lasted less than a half hour, but I was in anesthesia dreamland."

"How long before you could do it again?" Rocco asked from across the room,

"About six weeks."

"No pain?"

"Some discomfort the first couple of weeks after the operation, felt like heavy pressure on my scrotum, but when I laid on my back, everything felt fine. Some discomfort at the head of Big Gumba too at first, but that also went away. In fact, I'm more sensitive there now than I was as a young man."

"And how long can you keep it up?" Rocco asked to Brad's discomfort.

"As long as I want, paisan. Longer than you or this young man here. I just squeeze the little pump in my scrotum. That activates the device. The saline solution flows into my penis, and it stays up and rock-hard until I touch the pump again." Sal laughed. "My wife can jump me while I sleep, if she wants, by hitting that little pump. Told her, if I go first, she is to open my coffin, hit the pump, so I am hard when I get to hell and can screw the devil's wife!"

Elizabeth shook her head. "Brad and I, we're amazed and impressed at how freely Dr. Hakim's patients speak about their problems and the cures ... both women and men."

"That's 'cause we've never been happier with our sex lives. Hey, Rocco, I don't even need to be horny to get it up. I could hit the pump now and then become horny." He smiled at Elizabeth. "Nothing to worry about, young lady. You're safe for now."

"I'm curious ... my grandfather might need something like that," Elizabeth said. "What exactly is the penile prosthesis?"

"Careful," Brad said, "you may learn more than you want to know."

"Believe me, I already have."

FORTY-FIVE

Fixing The Problem: The Role Of Penile Prostheses

Implantation of a penile prosthesis is an effective treatment option which "fixes" the problem in all men with organic ED. Especially in men who have failed prior medical treatments, a penile prosthesis allows them to achieve a rigid erection spontaneously, any time, any place. Hence, we tell all our patients that even if medications fail, as long as they have a penis, we can get it hard for them.

Currently, the cost of a penile prosthesis (all types) ranges from $3,000 to $5,000. The good news is that for organic ED based on diagnostic testing most health insurance or Medicare will often cover the expense.

Various types of penile implants are currently available for use, including malleable or semi-rigid implants and inflatable devices. The malleable type device creates an erection that is always firm or hard without drugs or external aids. It is easily bent upward for sexual relations or bent downward, to be hidden out of the way when not in use. The malleable implants are completely

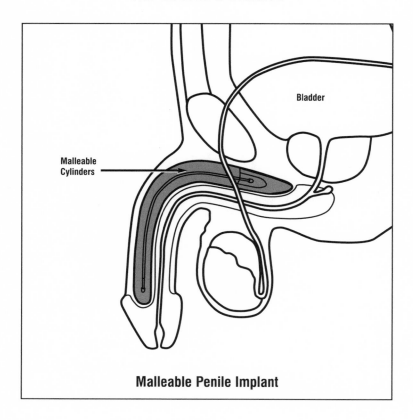

Malleable Penile Implant

concealed and should not interfere with pleasurable sensation, orgasm or ejaculation.

◆ ◆ ◆

Two companies in the United States, American Medical Systems and the Mentor Corporation, both in Minnesota currently produce/manufacture inflatable penile implants. The inflatable penile prosthesis (IPP) is highly effective in all types of erectile dysfunction with a 95 percent success rate at 5 years. It offers the highest satis-

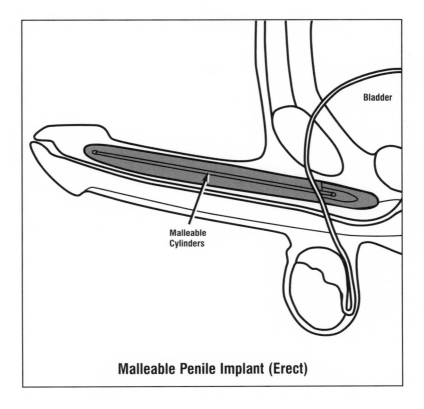

Malleable Penile Implant (Erect)

faction among patients and their partners when compared to all other ED treatments.

A recent study of 120 patients undergoing a Non-Nerve Sparing Radical Prostatectomy and IPP (combined) showed that the patients were able to *resume sexual intercourse at six weeks*! All patients reported improved psychological feelings of well-being and quality of life.

Yes, IPP offers the patient a spontaneous, natural-feeling erection, and it is totally concealed. This outpatient procedure is performed through a tiny opening in the scrotum or sac, with local or spinal anesthesia and currently takes a mere 30-40 minutes on average for the complete procedure.

Its potential disadvantages are minimal — a 1 to 3 percent rate of infection, as seen in any type of elective surgery, and a 2 to 3 percent malfunction rate, which is easily remedied.

Overall, it is *the* most effective alternative for men who are not satisfied with medical treatment and want to resume normal sexual function. The penile implant offers couples a permanent solution to a permanent problem.

Currently, inflatable penile prostheses are offered in either 2-piece or 3-piece designs. Two-piece inflatable implants, the AMS AMBICOR® device, provide an effective option for men with organic erectile dysfunction. They are especially useful in men after major pelvic surgery or after renal transplant. In my opinion, any man with ED and poor manual dexterity may benefit from this implant, which provides relatively simple inflation and deflation, with excellent rigidity. However, compared to a 3-piece device, the amount of flaccidity (softness) in the resting state is less natural. Also there is a lesser ability to enhance penile girth during erection.

The Mentor Alpha-1® and AMS 700cx® are both 3-piece inflatable penile prosthetic implants. They are saline-filled hydraulic devices that allow a patient to simulate a completely natural erection and flaccid state. The components consist of a saline reservoir, two penile cylinders placed in the penis, and a small pump apparatus placed in the scrotum, or sac, and are *completely hidden inside the body*. This device allows for an increase in both penile girth and rigidity when inflated, as well as excellent flaccidity when compared to 2-piece or malleable devices.

The advantages of the Mentor Alpha-1 are its construction from a sturdy bioflex polymer, extremely high reliability and low malfunction rate (less than 3 percent), and a single connector on the low-pressure portion of the device.

A Mentor Alpha-1 "narrow-based" device is also available for men with a history of severe scarring and fibrosis, or prior priapism. A "lock-out valve" reservoir design allows for greater patient comfort by preventing "autoinflation" or involuntary filling of the device. A re-

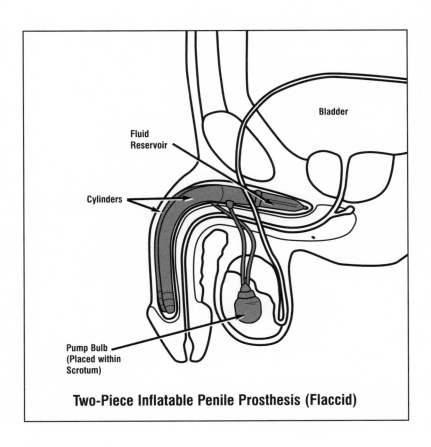

Two-Piece Inflatable Penile Prosthesis (Flaccid)

cent advance includes "a non-adherent" coating (aka Resist™) on the device to further decrease any chance of infection.

An advantage of the AMS 700CX device is it allows for "controlled expansion" of its silicone cylinders, making it especially useful in certain cases of corporal weakening and re-operation. A new antibiotic coating (Inhibizone™) could help decrease the risk of infection even more, and a new "cylinder" coating may improve device reliability.

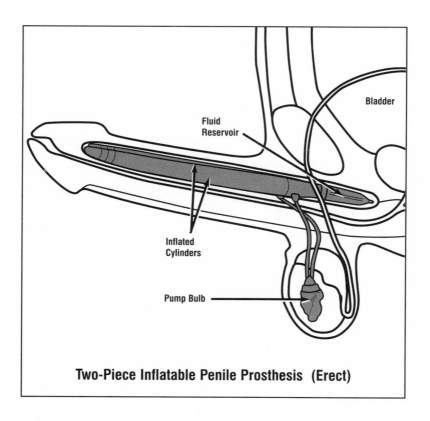

Bladder

Fluid Reservoir

Inflated Cylinders

Pump Bulb

Two-Piece Inflatable Penile Prosthesis (Erect)

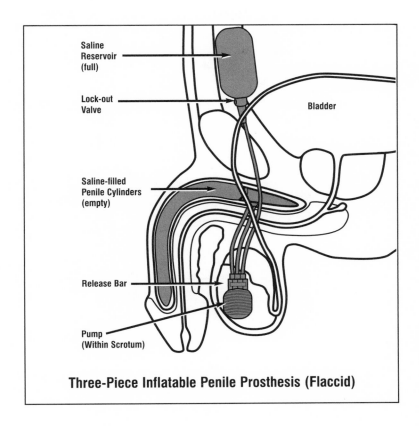

Saline Reservoir (full)

Lock-out Valve

Bladder

Saline-filled Penile Cylinders (empty)

Release Bar

Pump (Within Scrotum)

Three-Piece Inflatable Penile Prosthesis (Flaccid)

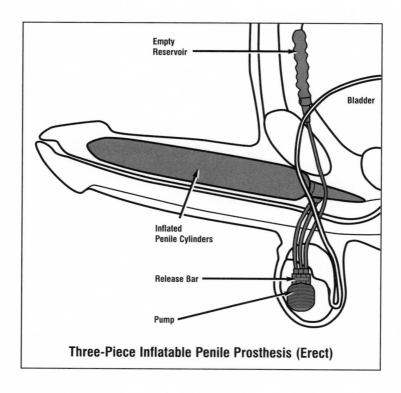

Empty Reservoir

Bladder

Inflated Penile Cylinders

Release Bar

Pump

Three-Piece Inflatable Penile Prosthesis (Erect)

20. Dr. Hakim's Waiting Room

"They look like they've had a nooner," Elizabeth said to Brad.

He glanced up from the magazine he'd been thumbing through. "Who?"

"That couple over at the reception counter."

"How can you tell?"

"By the glow on their faces ... the way they're giggling."

Brad took a longer look at the young couple. They were in their mid to late twenties he surmised. Both had a healthy out-doors look and were lean and trim in their shirts and jeans. "Yeah, he's got quite a satisfied smirk."

"How long before they engage us in conversation?" Elizabeth said.

"Momentarily ... they've made eye-contact."

"Hi," the young woman said to Elizabeth. "First time here?"

"Yes. And you?"

"Oh, no! I'm Rita and this is my husband, Eric."

"Elizabeth ... and my husband, Brad. Which of you had the problem?"

"We both did," Rita replied.

"Yeah," Eric said. "Doc always says it's a couples problem no matter who has the dysfunction. Actually it was my problem to begin with. I had a bike accident when I was young, and it was taking a long time to get even a partial erection. I was lucky if I could sustain it for as long as ten minutes."

"As much as we love each other, it was hurting our marriage."

"So you saw Dr. Hakim," Elizabeth said.

233

"Not right away," Eric said. "It was only after countless tests of having my Mr. Lucky poked, prodded, and inflated by numerous doctors and nurses that I saw Dr. Hakim."

"What did he do for you?" Brad asked.

"I had a microvascular arterial bypass … like they do with the heart … only it was for my Mr. Lucky."

Rita affectionately squeezed her husband's hand. "It was rough on Eric at first … for both of us."

"Yeah, and a complicated procedure. Doc took an artery from my abdomen and rerouted it down to Mr. Lucky, where he connected it under a microscope. Took a few hours, I was told."

Brad felt as if **his** testicles suddenly had retractable landing gears. "How long were you in the hospital? A week or two?"

"No, just overnight. A couple of days after the operation, Rita took me off the pain killers 'cause she thought I was becoming a zombie. Then when I went back to work, I moved, sat, and rose very slowly. Not that I was surprised, but time dragged during the healing process. Doc told me not to use Mr. Lucky for at least six to eight weeks and not to expect it to be healed for a few months."

"It was a tough time for both of us," Rita said.

"Just like the doctor told me, by three months, we were getting back to our normal sex life. It's been two years since the surgery. Everything works fine. I'm a new man!"

"Then you think the pain and length of time to recover was worth it," Elizabeth said.

"It's been wonderful," Rita said. "Sometimes he lasts longer than I do."

Eric kissed his wife. "The operation saved our marriage too."

Elizabeth turned to speak to Brad, but he had picked up his magazine again.

FORTY-SIX

Microvascular Arterial Bypass Surgery

In selected men, microvascular arterial bypass surgery will provide improved erectile blood flow and rigidity during sexual stimulation, that is, a more rigid, more spontaneous penile erection. This surgery is generally recommended only for younger men without systemic risk factors, whose erectile dysfunction has been caused by blunt perineal injury. It restores "normal" arterial blood flow to the penis, similar to heart bypass, in 70 percent of cases.

Impotent patients with systemic atherosclerotic disease are typically poor candidates for microvascular arterial bypass surgery. So are those with other generalized arterial occlusive diseases secondary to systemic vascular risk factors such as aging, hypertension, cigarette smoking, diabetes mellitus and hypercholesterolemia, and others with an associated veno-occlusive dysfunction or "leakage" problem.

The patient's primary motivation for penile microvascular arterial bypass surgery is his desire to restore his natural erectile function and achieve sexually stimulated spontaneous rigid erections without the need for external or internal mechanical devices, pills or penile injections of vasoactive agents.

Carefully selected young patients with pure arteriogenic impotence ("failure to fill") who have many years of sexuality ahead of them if possible will always desire the natural restoration of normal erectile function.

Put simply, patients with pure arteriogenic impotence due to a blocked artery can be described as having "failure to fill" or cavernosal artery insufficiency. They often lose the slowly developing partial erection during preparatory sexual stimulation, just prior to or soon after penetration, as a result of anxiety, or stress response.

A critical factor in achieving success with microvascular arterial bypass surgery is strict patient selection. The sexual history of the ideal candidate for such surgery would be a young man with slowly developing or poorly spontaneous, weak erections during sexual activity that typically developed after some sort of injury.

These patients characteristically have the ability to achieve a more rigid, longer lasting erection during sleep or upon awakening in the morning. The ability to sustain the morning erection reflects the fact that such patients have underlying normal corporal veno-occlusive function, or "storage of blood".

In this unique population of impotent men with pure arterial insufficiency due to trauma, the microvascular arterial bypass procedure will achieve improved, longstanding erectile function in 2 of 3 patients.

Erectile function tests should be performed in those who wish to pursue microvascular arterial bypass surgery, which is also known as Penile Revascularization Surgery.

Rarely will preoperative complications occur during the erectile function testing.

The most reliable preoperative tests to examine penile blood flow are Duplex Doppler ultrasonography and dynamic infusion pharmaco-cavernosometry and cavernosography, or DICC testing. That is followed by selective pudendal arteriography of the penile and pelvic arteries, which provides us with an internal roadmap of the blood flow and associated blockage.

The specific objective of this surgery is to provide an alternative arterial inflow pathway, an "end run" if you will, beyond the blockage in the arterial supply to the erection. That is best achieved by designing the vascular reconstruction to the patient's specific arteriographic findings.

Microvascular arterial bypass surgery is technically demanding. The internal diameters of the recipient blood vessels are often between a mere 0.5 to 0.7 millimeters. Suture material used for the reconnection of veins and arteries (anastomosis) is typically 10-0 nylon, smaller and narrower than a human hair, which is applied during surgery under the control of the operating microscope.

FORTY-SEVEN

Premature Ejaculation

Premature ejaculation (PE) a condition that affects millions of men, occurs when the male ejaculates within one or two minutes (or less) of entering the vagina and is too quick for his partner's satisfaction. This leads to further problems with increased anxiety and worsening of erections as well. In some cases, ejaculation occurs even prior to penetration.

I like to consider PE as being divided into two distinct types, primary and secondary PE. Secondary PE, which is often a result of ED, typically occurs after the male notices difficulty sustaining an erection. In this case, he may ejaculate much sooner than his partner would like, almost as if he knows that if he does not ejaculate quickly he won't be able to sustain his erection. As a result, his partner will be unable to reach orgasm and be left unsatisfied, which worsens the couple's problems.

This often leads to a cycle of increased anxiety and sexual dysfunction. In evaluating a male who has premature ejaculation, we must also assess the underlying causes of his ED.

The primary form of premature ejaculation can occur in men who have normal erections and find that immediately upon penetration of the vagina they ejaculate, usually in less than one or two minutes. Some of these men can sustain an erection longer during masturbation as long as there is no continuous stimulation. In these cases, PE may be due to hypersensitivity or other neurologic changes in the glans, although it may also be due to psychological causes. Performance anxiety can lead to a vicious cycle. Other physical causes that can lead to premature ejaculation include infections of the prostate and bladder.

Once a diagnosis of premature ejaculation has been made, certain treatments can be very effective. Sex therapy can reduce performance anxiety, as well as learning 'stop-start' techniques where just before the "point of no return" he stops any sexual stimulation. Gradually he starts again, and some men can be taught to hold back or delay ejaculation. The "squeeze" technique is also used in sex therapy where a man or his partner learns to squeeze the head or base of the penis just before the point of no return and that will often prevent ejaculation for the time being.

Various medications have been shown to improve or delay time to orgasm. It was noticed that many men taking SSRI-antidepressant agents suffered delayed ejaculation as a side-effect of their treatment for depression. This "side-effect" was then applied to men who had premature ejaculation. By taking regular limited doses of SSRI-antidepressants, they could delay their time to ejaculation, especially when combined with the sex therapy techniques previously described. Other treatment options may include topical anesthetic creams, condom usage, or even a first ejaculation prior to intercourse in younger men with a short refractory period.

Any man experiencing ED and premature ejaculation should know that once a proper diagnosis is made effective treatments are available.

FORTY-EIGHT

Priapism

Priapism, named after Priapus, the mythological Greek god of fertility and the chief deity of lasciviousness and obscenity, is a very dangerous male sexual dysfunction, which left untreated can lead to permanent impotency. After Priapus' mother Aphrodite was cursed by Hera, he was made a dwarf with an enormous phallus that was represented fully erect on his images and statues.

Priapism typically describes a condition whereby a male develops an unwanted prolonged sustained erection, often lasting greater than 3 hours. It is usually *not* caused by erotic stimulation or sexual desire. Orgasm or ejaculation will not relieve the erection even when it results from sexual stimulation. Any delay in seeking medical assistance may minimize a successful outcome, which can then lead to permanent impotence. Although uncommon, cases of priapism in *women* (clitoral priapism) have been reported after use of certain medications, including Trazodone®.

HOW DOES A MALE DEVELOP PRIAPISM?

Priapism is associated with a number of causes, including sickle cell anemia, use of cocaine, use of medications that cause erections such as Trazodone, and overdoses of self-injection therapy for ED. It can also be caused by blunt penile and perineal injury leading to a condition referred to as arterial or "high flow" priapism.

WARNING! If a male takes cocaine, he can develop priapism and end up in the hospital for a necessary operation to reverse the problem and in severe cases may be rendered permanently impotent.

The overall success of treatments for priapism to restore long-term potency has been disappointing. The proper and immediate diagnosis by a qualified urologist is critical to assure the best outcome and increased chances of remaining potent.

21. Dr. Hakim's Waiting Room

A young man came in and sat down next to Brad. "Hi, we look about the same age. Name is Michael, 34 years old."

"Brad." Here we go again, he whispered to Elizabeth.

"Pretty young for both of us to have a problem."

"And yours is?"

"Ever hear of Peyronie's Disease?"

"Is it one of those Sexually Transmitted Diseases, what my dad calls VD?"

"Oh, God, no. I've got severe curvature of the penis." He gestured towards Elizabeth. "Hope I'm not offending you."

"No, I've heard more extreme stuff since we've been here."

"Well, I've no problem getting erect, nor do I experience pain, but I can't penetrate a woman due to the curvature..."

Brad raised his eyebrows. "Wow!"

"... and my GP recommended I see Dr. Hakim."

"What do you think he'll do?" Elizabeth asked.

"I don't know, but I sure hope he can cure me."

"What causes it?" Brad said.

"I know one thing that does," an African American in his forties said seated nearby. "About three years ago, I got injured while having sex with my wife. Don't ask me how. Afterwards, I developed a 60-degree curvature of my penis and what the doctor called mild bottlenecking. Unfortunately, because of the curvature my wife complained of discomfort during intercourse."

Michael looked down at his crotch. "What did the doctor suggest?"

243

"After trying vitamin E, Potaba, Colchicine, Verapamil and even a 12-week course of intralesional interferon, the bottlenecking problem was resolved, but I've still got a persistent 40-degree curvature that bothers my wife and I, making intercourse difficult. So I'm back now to get it fixed."

FORTY-NINE

Peyronie's Disease

Most women and men have been unaware of another potency-threatening condition of male ED, Peyronie's Disease. The symptoms may be immediately obvious: A curved or bent penis, penile plaque, decreased penile length, diminished penile stretch, less rigidity, and erectile dysfunction. This is different than "congenital" curvature of the penis as seen in children and young adults.

The causes of Peyronie's Disease or penile curvature can vary and are not always known in every situation. Most commonly it is caused by solitary or repeated injury during sexual activity. This injury leads to scarring, the forming of plaque, and loss of elasticity or "stretch" in the lining of the penis or tunica albuginea.

During sex, typically with his partner on top, a man can also "break" his penis ("broken penis syndrome"), which is essentially a corporal fracture. True, there is no "bone" to fracture in the erect penis; instead, in this case, fracture refers to an injury or tearing in the erectile body of the penis.

MRI studies (Magnetic Resonance Imaging) suggest that a force on the erect penis in or against the vagina

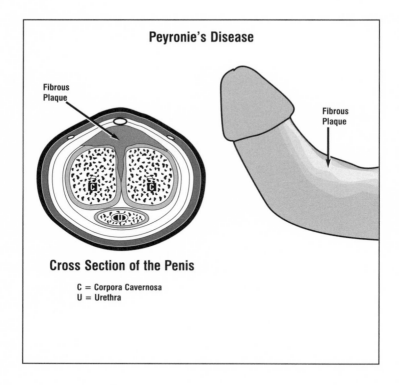

during sexual activities commonly causes trauma to the lining of the penis (tunica albuginea) that results in scarring, plaque formation, penile curvature, and even erectile dysfunction.

Injury may also occur when a man accidentally withdraws from his partner still erect, or his penis hits his partner's pubic bone during thrusting. Various patients have suffered trauma when, with enough force, their erect penis accidentally smashed against the nightstand, floor, bedpost, or even the bathroom door. Despite the cause, corporal fracture can cause bleeding, pain and swelling, and typically is a medical emergency. If treated early with surgical repair, normal sexual function may return. When a major injury occurs, however, and there is no early treatment, then permanent scarring and plaque may form leading to severe curvature of the penis with poor erectile function possibly requiring a penile prosthesis.

Some patients have Peyronie's Disease in association with other abnormalities. One of these is Dupuytren's Contracture, found in certain types of arthritis, resulting in curving of the finger. Peyronie's Disease or penile curvature has also been reported following prostate surgery.

Typically, the curvature is in the direction of the plaque, which usually forms on the dorsal or backside of the penis, the side a man is looking at when his penis is erect. When the penis engorges, if erection is not affected, it bends backward towards the plaque due to the lack of elasticity on that side.

To get a mental picture of this, imagine a long balloon you see at the circus or fairgrounds. Typically, when you blow it up it goes out straight. Now stick a piece of masking tape on one side of the balloon and then blow it up. The tape prevents the balloon from stretching on that side; hence it curves *towards* the masking tape. In effect, the plaque acts on the penis as the masking tape does on the balloon.

Although one of the main symptoms of Peyronie's Disease is penile curvature, other common symptoms can include pain and numbness due to inflammation involving the nerves of the penis. Also, loss of penile length may occur due to its lack of elasticity or stretch.

Peyronie's Disease can cause poor erectile function. The penis may become firm up to the point of the plaque and remain soft beyond that point. In these instances, the patient may see a narrowing "bottleneck" or an "hour-glass" shape of the penis as well. The plaque can also prevent the penis from storing blood during erection. As a result, the patient may have an inability to have intercourse because of a soft and curved penis.

After an appropriate diagnosis is made and vascular testing performed, the physician will prescribe treatment tailored to the individual. Watchful waiting is one option. For some, the disease resolves itself completely and stabilizes after 6 to 12 months without invasive treatment. However, once the plaque is stable or calcified, more invasive treatments may be needed, especially if severe curvature or ED continues to prevent satisfactory intercourse.

Various therapeutic options are available for patients who have Peyronie's Disease, including medical and surgical intervention. Conservative medical treatments include antioxidants such as Vitamin E, Potaba, and Colchicine, an anti-gout medicine that has been shown to improve inflammation. If these medicines are taken daily during the acute stage of the process, they may play some role in improving the outcome. Medications can be applied topically as well as injected directly into the scars or plaque, such as with interferon, verapamil or steroids.

Current clinical trials are further investigating the use of interferon and verapamil as intralesional therapies. However significant benefits and plaque resolution remain to be shown in all except the least severe cases.

Radiation treatments for Peyronie's Disease have been reported in medical literature, but this treatment should be avoided as it can worsen the overall function of the penis. It is mentioned here only to be condemned.

Surgical intervention is usually not viewed as an option until the condition has stabilized, usually after 6-12 months. At that point if there is still significant penile curvature and sexual dysfunction, surgery may be an option.

To restore a straight erection with normal sexual function, a number of effective procedures can be used, including Nesbit Plication, or plaque incision and grafting.

For patients who have poor erectile function, insertion of a penile implant with subsequent repair of any residual curvature is an excellent treatment option for restoring both normal sexual function and a straight erection.

Setting realistic goals is essential prior to any form of therapy. Numbness and loss of length do not always improve or resolve despite any type of therapeutic intervention. Patients with Peyronie's Disease must understand all the possibilities. Although excellent treatment options are available, each person needs to be diagnosed and evaluated individually by a doctor who is an expert in this area because no one treatment is appropriate for everyone.

◆ ◆ ◆

A penile lesion, which may be confused with Peyronie's Disease or plaque, is "sclerosing lymphangitis" (S.L.). S.L. is a superficial ropelike lesion, usually located at the "coronal sulcus" or backside of the penile shaft. It is most commonly seen in men who engage in extremely vigorous sex and is thought to be due to repeated penile trauma during intercourse. A "thrombosed" vein (not actually lymphatic) is felt anatomically, which usually and spontaneously returns to normal after a period of abstinence. Evaluation by a physician may be necessary to make a proper diagnosis.

22. Dr. Hakim's Office

"Brad, I wish you'd brought me your medical records."

"I didn't know what to expect, doctor. Anyway, I haven't had a physical since I left college, and those were for sports. Don't have the time."

"You should be examined at least once a year. Now then, do you think you have a problem with your sexual function?"

"Well, I've thought about having one of those lengthening procedures. I can always use a few extra inches."

"To use a bridge term, I'm asking you about strength rather than length. Are you having problems with your erections during lovemaking and sexual intercourse?"

"Sometimes ... recently ... I guess Elizabeth senses that too. Also my desire for sex has gone down lately."

"What about your morning or night time erections?"

"You mean pee hard-ons?"

"Yes."

"They've actually been pretty good. Better than my recent sex erections, in fact."

"Elizabeth told me you changed jobs. Starting up your own law firm. Think you're experiencing more stress than usual?"

"I don't know, but I really want to make our relationship work."

"That's a great attitude."

"So, doc, what do you think is the cause of my problem?"

"Could be a number of things ... low testosterone ... poor blood flow ... stress ..."

"Not me!"

"... *or performance anxiety. Once a male fails in the bed-room, he often fears it might happen again. It can become a vicious cycle. As he starts to* **worry** *about his erection, the adrena-line starts flowing, during what we call a sympathetic nerve response or fight-or-flight response. Adrenaline acts as a smooth-muscle constrictor, so the penis arteries narrow and the tissues can't expand, and your erection goes down.*"

"*So, I'm already starting behind the 8-ball,*" *Brad said.*

"*Yes, in fact, this type of SD can also lead to poor libido or decreased desire for sex. Just imagine if every time you got up to the plate, you struck out. After a while, you'd give up baseball.*" *Dr. Hakim showed Brad a chart. "Aside from the reason that brought you here, it would be wise for you to undergo a complete exam to make sure there is nothing wrong with you physically.*"

"*Now?*"

"*Yes, I want to check out a few things. After that, I want to speak to both of you. Can you and Elizabeth stay a while longer? I've got several patients waiting for me in the exam rooms.*"

251

FIFTY

If Looks Could Thrill! Phalloplasty And Penile Cosmetic Surgery

Another issue related to SD in men is a desire for penile lengthening and thickening, which is heavily advertised in the media including pornographic magazines, on Internet web sites, and unasked for e-mail. That controversial issue is also being debated in the medical community regarding augmentation "phalloplasty" or surgical penile enlargement therapy.

Doctors are asking many questions. What are the strategies? Are they beneficial? Is it desirable? What can patients expect realistically, and should they even consider this option?

In fact many men seeking this therapy are found to have a completely normal penis. Going back to the 1960s, Masters and Johnson commented on the history of many cultures in which they believed the size of the penis, flaccid or erect, reflected the sexual prowess of the male.

Even the best educated and affluent believe that penis size equates with power and virility.

In fact, if you ask any male if he would like to have a smaller penis, the resounding answer would be NO! Despite the number of women who undergo breast enhancement surgery, many women with very large breasts, when asked if they would like to have theirs reduced in size, will say yes! And many do undergo breast reduction surgery. Have you ever heard of any male asking for "penis reduction surgery"?

Over the past 20 years, we have seen a dramatic upswing in all levels of cosmetic surgery from the basic "nose job," face-lift, and skin peel to total body transformation. As a result, a new surgical specialty deals with lengthening and expanding the girth of the penis.

To-date, several procedures have been developed. Some techniques are not all that new and are based on well-established pediatric surgery techniques for congenital problems such as micro-penis. It addition fat and fat grafts have been used by plastic surgeons for many years. So, many of these procedures were combined.

Many patients have rushed to have these procedures performed in the eternal quest for a larger penis, and many unrealistic promises have been made. Unfortunately, problems can occur and results may be less than optimum. Emotional problems stemming from that disappointment as well as physical difficulties leading to sexual dysfunction can result from these procedures.

Also, insurance often does not cover the high cost of surgery and this seriously impacts on the pocketbook of the disappointed patient.

The various professional societies that study impotence and are part of the American Urological Association have issued position statements on the various procedures. They have stated that "phalloplasty" is experimental and long-term safety and efficacy are not yet proven.

One of the ethical issues is that many of these patients have a penis in the normal size range with no abnormalities or pathologies. The typical patient who undergoes phalloplasty is heterosexual with a normal penis that is 5 to 6 inches when erect. For such men, phalloplasty will not enhance sexual function. It is merely cosmetic surgery. Even if the patient ignores the fact of his normality and demands the surgery, *ethically* how can a physician justify this type of operation on normal men?

Of course, the other side of the issue is when a person decides to have a nose job or breast enhancement. Will ethical cosmetic surgeons decide no in certain cases? If there is a problem of self-esteem among the patients, the cosmetic surgeon will usually go ahead with the operation because that is the rationale of most cosmetic therapies — except in case of disfigurement caused by birth, accident, or disease such as breast cancer.

One might say that male fixation on the size of his penis is analogous to that of an unnaturally thin woman who looks in the mirror and still sees herself as overweight.

The same can hold true for those whose low self-esteem may date from their first public shower in the boy's gym. Prudent behavior would dictate that they see a psychiatrist first.

One cause for male preoccupation with "length" is suspected to be pornography, which causes the men to measure themselves against the performers.

Typical surgical enhancement involves division of those ligaments that suspend and support the penis. All it does is allow the penis to lie more forward or hang down, about an inch or so more in its flaccid or soft state, an illusion of lengthening, if you will. This procedure does *not* lengthen the penis when it is fully erect.

Many who perform this operation say they have the patient use a weighted device attached to the penis for 3 to 6 months after surgery to prevent shrinkage to normal or even *smaller* size, due to scarring.

How do surgeons address girth or wideness of the penis, which supposedly gives more sexual satisfaction to women than length? Girth is done through liposuction girth enhancement procedures or fat grafts in which fat is taken from the patient's abdomen and transferred to the penis. Early attempts led to uneven absorption of the fat leaving bumps and such that were cosmetically undesirable. Also shrinkage occurred due to absorption of water from the fat cells. But if the fat graft has a blood supply, then absorption is less likely. Currently, innovations such as fat injections may give a cosmetically aesthetic look to the penis and regain some lost girth. Other options to increase girth include the use of cadaver tissue, which some surgeons believe can lead to satisfactory results. Patients who should not undergo these treatments include those who feel it will improve urination, fertility, erections, or ejaculations.

Peer review has led to the creation of professional societies to oversee phalloplasty procedures. The American Academy of Phalloplastic Surgeons is one. They have imposed accountability requiring pre- and post-operative evaluations and standardization.

AAPS currently states that phalloplasty patients can expect an increase of approximately 2 to 3 centimeters in length, and 1 to 2 centimeters in diameter of the penis *in the flaccid state*. Of course these results may vary and complications can occur including necrosis, scarring, and loss of length.

Again, it must be emphasized that strict criteria should govern these procedures. True, certain select patients with micro-penises may benefit from phalloplasty, but they are not that common among adults. After childbirth, hidden or buried penis is relatively infrequent.

In February 2001, a relevant story on the subject of phalloplasty circulated on the Internet. The Brazilian Institute for Sexual Health (*Instituto Brasileiro para Saúde Sexual*) was inundated with questions relating to penile length and thickness. Researchers from Rio Grande do Sul and California reported that the average penile length for a Brazilian male is 14.5 cm (5.7 inches) as opposed to 12.9 cm (5.1 inches) for the United States.

Brazilian doctors will recommend penile lengthening only in rare cases, when the male's penis is less than 7 cm (2.7 inches). The operation, which is considered experimental and must be performed at a university hospital, requires special approval from the Federal Medicine Board and generally adds a maximum of 2-cm (0.8 inches) to the penis.

In 2000, the Brazilian Health Ministry approved an extensor to lengthen the penis a few centimeters, which also requires a medical procedure.

◆ ◆ ◆

Another reason for a patient to undergo phalloplasty is the need for Transgender surgery, which is a serious matter in the context of sexual function as well as identity and personal well-being. Contrary to most popular and even bigoted opinions, some of these surgeries are necessary because of mistakes made by physicians and parents when a child is born with both male and female, or incomplete sexual characteristics.

A female or male forced to live as one of the opposite gender because of such an incorrect, early decision may be an excellent candidate for this type of reconstructive surgery, which includes phalloplasty *and* penile implants as well as extended consultations with a psychiatrist and sex therapist. The complex surgical techniques are better left for another book.

PART VI

COMPLEMENTARY AND ALTERNATIVE MEDICINE AND SEXUAL FUNCTION

FIFTY-ONE

Herbals And Other Alternate Therapies

The use of herbals and other alternative medications is becoming a preferred choice of therapy for many in the United States. Americans spend in excess of 30 billion dollars a year on supplemental products. They see complementary and alternative medicine practitioners more often than they do primary care physicians.

Because of the public's great interest in complementary and alternative medicine (CAM), in March 2000, President Clinton signed an executive order establishing a White House Commission of thirteen physicians, which grew to twenty with the addition of those specializing in homeopathic and alternative medicines. The purpose was to provide the President with information and recommendations and create a policy to maximize the benefits of CAM. The commission focused on education and training of practitioners as well as research into alternative medicine practices and products. They also looked at ways to generate public access to the information and products, and discover if these therapies can/ will be covered by insurance.

Also in March 2001, Harvard Medical School (HMS) invited candidates to apply for a three-year National Institutes of Health funded fellowship in Complementary and Alternative Medicine (CAM) Research and Education for 2002. Then in May 2001, HMS announced receipt of a 10-million dollar gift from the Bernard Osher Foundation to study non-traditional medicine. Associate Professor of Medicine David M. Eisenberg, who became interested in alternative medicine while visiting China, is the Director of the HMS Division for Research and Education in Complementary and Integrative Medicine.

Of note, Columbia University has had since 1993 The Rosenthal Center for Contemporary and Alternative Medicine and a Center for CAM Research in Women's Health. Typically, at the time of writing this book, The Rosenthal Center was seeking "healthy" menopausal women for a study on herbal treatment for hot flashes. 50 percent were to receive the herb Black Cohosh and 50 percent a placebo in the blind study.

Along with an increasing number of major medical schools, both Harvard and Columbia Medical Schools are intensifying their validated studies in the efficacy of herbals and nutraceuticals in treating ailments. Specific research from Stanford University is covered in the chapter on Nutritional Supplements and FSD.

The issue of CAM becomes interesting because more complementary and alternative therapies are currently being recommended by physicians as well, including herbal products and nutraceuticals for afflictions such as enlarged prostate (Saw Palmetto), prostatitis (Prosta-Q), and other medical diseases. Many believe we are now only seeing the tip of the iceberg for the beneficial use of these treatments, herbal products, and nutraceuticals, and we can expect this knowledge to expand greatly over the next few years.

Recent studies have shown that sexual function may be improved, especially for women, by using alternative medical therapies and herbal treatments.

Although controversial, a number of herbals are reported to improve arousal, sexual response, sexual sensation, and sexual function in men and women through increased blood flow and facilitation of sexual performance.

They may also act upon the sexual response as aphrodisiacs and affect different stages of sexual response. They can increase blood flow to the genitalia, relieve stress, and produce a general feeling of well-being. By taking certain substances regularly, patients hope to increase sexual drive, sensitivity in the genital area, and achieve increased performance.

Be aware, however, unlike drugs or pharmaceuticals, herbs vary in strength, purity, and effectiveness. Variations in body processing, storage, and dosages *are not* always standardized. They need to be obtained from reputable labs, and consumers should read labels carefully. With few exceptions, herbals are not approved (or condemned) by the Food and Drug Administration.

The important and effective herbal ingredients, which will be discussed in the next chapters, should serve as a reference for those seeking to utilize these therapies for improved sexual health. Attention to purity is critical, however, when buying these supplements, as they are not FDA approved or monitored for their intended use. Look for an "analysis" of purity whenever available, to assure what you are taking is really what you expect.

FIFTY-TWO

Aphrodisiacs And Dangerous Herbals

Perhaps even in pre-history, humans began their relentless search for the ultimate herbal aphrodisiac. Over centuries they have tried everything and anything to restore the peak sexual prowess of their youth. Some have been absurd, nothing more than placebos or primitive transference of animal genitalia. Others have been and still are dangerous.

Often, reliance upon the efficacy of certain aphrodisiacs is a cultural matter, even among the educated. How many friends do you have who believe in the power of raw oysters as a way to improve their sexual function?

Belief "exotic is better" has produced testimonials to ancient remedies such as camel hump fat, jackal bile, or the fungus in China that grows on dormant worms, *dong chong xia cao*.

Today, in Hangzhou and other major cities in China, one can find street vendors hawking Tiger penis for about twenty dollars a thumb's width, which must be soaked in brandy for a month before being ingested. They might

264

recommend monkey member as well, although all wish they had one from the rhinoceros. People being what they are, unscrupulous vendors will substitute burro or ox for the true desired product, the efficacy of which in all cases is still unproven.

What follows is an unbiased description of various common herbal products in use today that some claim *may be* efficacious in restoring sexual vigor.

◆ ◆ ◆

Damiana is a small shrub found in North America used as an aphrodisiac by both women and men. It has been prescribed to treat women with low libido and is taken about an hour before making love.

Men also have used Damiana to treat their sexual dysfunction. When combined with another herb indigenous to Florida, Saw Palmetto, it is recommended for certain problems connected with the prostate.

It has been suggested that Damiana contains alkaloids similar to caffeine, which may have stimulating and alkaloid effects that increase blood flow to the genital area generating more sensitivity. Damiana has also been reported to regulate hormone activity, and some people using it claim to have had a reaction of mild euphoria lasting up to a few hours.

Ginkgo Biloba is said to increase blood flow to the genitals by relaxing the walls of blood vessels. Taken daily and an hour before sexual activity, it is reported to be a fast-acting aphrodisiac.

The Chinese have used Ginkgo for thousands of years to increase sexual vitality, promote longevity, and cure various ailments. It improves blood flow to vital organs without raising blood pressure. It is believed to positively affect the aging process because many problems amongst the elderly are caused by poor blood circulation. As an example, inadequate blood flow to the brain may impair memory, lead to depression and strokes. That is why this herb has been recommended for patients suffering from memory loss.

Because Ginkgo Biloba also increases blood flow to the genitalia in women and men, it is recommended to be taken on a regular basis and before sexual activity. Studies over the past ten years have shown it may improve sexual dysfunction caused by vascular insufficiency to the penis.

In addition to improving blood flow, Ginkgo Biloba also contains an antioxidant, which protects the brain and other organs of the body from free radical damage.

Ginkgo Biloba is also known to be a blood thinner and *should not* be taken in conjunction with aspirin and other anticoagulant drugs.

Ginseng is an herb known as an energizer, revitalizer, and aphrodisiac. It is found in three varieties — Asian, Siberian, and American. The Chinese have literally translated it as *roots man*. Its appearance in Chinese medical literature dates back thousands of years. Its use as an aphrodisiac for the restoration of lovemaking stamina is well-documented.

The Asian variety is highly prized in India. Asian and American Ginseng have been reported to be effective as aphrodisiacs and adaptable to the requirements of an individual's body. Its substances allow it to adapt to the hormone needs of women as during menopause. At that time, it can increase their estrogen levels and may be useful in treating menopausal symptoms such as hot flashes.

Caution should be taken for those with hypertension and kidney disease or those taking anticoagulants or any blood thinner.

Kava Kava is an herbal reported to heighten sexuality and stimulate the genitalia. It can be taken less than an hour before sexual activity.

Alpha-pyrones in Kava Kava may help muscle relaxation, reduce anxiety and nervousness, and promote a warm, sociable feeling, and in some cases a state of relaxed euphoria.

Those who have Parkinson's disease or are taking certain antidepressants should *not* use Kava Kava.

Muira Puama (*potency wood*, as the natives call it) is a South American plant. Over the centuries, tribal healers made an extract from it to cure erectile dysfunction. It is still used in some cultures as an aphrodisiac and nerve stimulant. When this herb is taken over a period of a few weeks, patients report improvement in their sex drive, and men especially note an improvement in erectile problems. It can be taken as a tea or in capsule form a short time prior to lovemaking.

At the World Institute of Sexology in Paris, 262 men participated in a controlled study. They lacked sexual desire or could not achieve or sustain an erection. Half were given Muira Puama, the others a placebo for a two week period. As reported in *The American Journal of Natural Medicine*, 62 percent of those taking Muira Puama reported improvement in sexual function.

Yohimbine is derived from the bark of the yohimbe tree. Many cultures claim it has aphrodisiac effects that enhance sexual function. The active ingredient is yohim-bine hydrochloride, an alkaloid.

Yohimbine induces blood vessel dilation in the penis. Studies have shown an increase in sexual potency amongst men who have diabetes and cardiovascular disease, especially when they take Yohimbine combined with other herbal substances on a regular basis.

Individuals who have kidney disease, hypertension, and psychological problems must take care if they use Yohimbine. It should not be taken with substances and foods that contain tyramine, an amino acid, because the combo can raise blood pressure. That includes cheeses, red wine, and certain diet aids.

Other reportedly useful herbal substances include:

Saw Palmetto is an herbal noted for its efficacy in the treatment of disorders of the prostate — enlargement, obstruction, and prostatitis. Saw Palmetto comes from a shrub found along the southeastern coast of North America. It is a fan shaped herb that resembles a palm. The red and brown berries of the Saw Palmetto plant are used also by women and men to improve sexual vigor. Its possible effects include use as a diuretic and reduction of prostate inflammation.

Dong Quai has been used by women to improve their reproductive systems. It is a Chinese root that has been used for many generations, especially during the menstrual cycle to relieve menstrual pain, cramps, and symptoms of PMS. Dong Quai is rich in magnesium, vitamin B-12, vitamin E, and also stimulates secretion of the female sex hormone estrogen. Pregnant women are advised *not* to use it.

Multiform is a Chinese herbal used as a stimulant for sexual arousal. Its ability to activate penile erection has been revered by Chinese medicine for over 5,000 years. Its energy enhancing properties are said to encourage a more active sex life, especially in those patients who have poor adrenal function. This is especially important for those whose sexual dysfunction has been caused by anxiety and stress.

Wild Oats has been reported to be an aphrodisiac. Its use in Chinese herbal therapy goes back thousands of years. It is recorded that Chinese fish farmers who fed fish with these oats found them breeding more aggressively.

Skullcap, a tranquilizing herb reported to reduce stress and relax the nervous system.

Astragulus australus membranus is an herbal substance thought to improve sexual function by stepping up the metabolism. It is also reported to be a stimulant for the immune system.

Black Kohasch, from a plant indigenous to Eastern and North America, is an herb reported to rejuvenate the male sex organ and said to be successful in the treatment of erectile problems. It has been also shown to strengthen the female and male reproductive systems.

◆ ◆ ◆

Although the previously mentioned herbals when taken wisely *may* benefit women and men, other herbal substances may cause or worsen underlying medical problems and cause kidney failure or stroke. These herbals may in fact be severely toxic and even fatal and should be avoided or used with extreme caution.

Spanish Fly is reputedly an aphrodisiac that stimulates the penis and vagina. However, it is more likely to irritate and blister the genitalia and the mucus membrane of the genitourinary tract. This can lead to inflammation of the bladder and urethra causing unwanted painful erections in men and an equally unpleasant engorged clitoris in women. The kidneys may become inflamed, which can cause a burning sensation, and receive more serious damage. Spanish Fly can also cause coma. That is why it is classified as a *poison*.

Ma huang or **Ephedra** are herbs used in the past by Chinese for ailments such as asthma. They are currently touted as substitutes for recreational drugs such as Ecstasy for immediate sexual and euphoric feelings. However, Ephedra can cause irregular heartbeat, strokes, and cardiac arrest.

Jimson Weed is another dangerous intoxicating herbal that reportedly increases sex drive and produces a high, but it has also caused fatalities.

Marijuana, Cannabis is a narcotic reported to have aphrodisiac effects. It predominantly acts as a sedative, however, and can cause erectile and general sexual dysfunction and temporary sterility. It decreases potency in a similar fashion as alcohol and also decreases levels of testosterone in large amounts. Depending on the amount smoked, marijuana can lower a person's sex drive.

FIFTY-THREE

Nutritional Supplements, Validated Studies, And Female Sexual Function

A number of papers have been written about nutritional supplements that enhance female sexual function. Some have already been described such as Ginger Root, Ginkgo Biloba, Kava Kava, Yohimbe, Ginseng, Damiana, Vitamin E, and DHEA.

Others include L-arginine, Niacin, Rhodiola, Selenium, Schizandra, Wild Yam, Pycnogenol, a potent antioxidant, and Red Clover Extract for post-menopausal women. These products have not been approved by the FDA for the treatment of FSD.

◆ ◆ ◆

In 2000 at the International Female Sexual Dysfunction Meeting in Boston, researchers from Stanford University presented a double-blind study with placebo controls of nutritional supplements that enhance female sexual function.

The supplement tested consisted of extracts from Ginkgo Biloba, Korean Ginseng, Damiana, Calcium, Iron, L-arginine, Zinc, and multivitamins. The women ranged in age from 22 to 75. The study predominantly looked at those with decreased sexual desire and had them answer a validated questionnaire with a female sexual function index used in the past for the evaluation of Viagra.

The study also included the effect of supplements versus placebo on women who were pre-menopausal, peri-menopausal, and post-menopausal. Of note, the women who were peri-menopausal had the *most* significant improvement in sexual function. 73 percent reported *increased desire and satisfaction* in their sexual relationships, and 75 percent had *improved clitoral sensation.*

67 percent of pre-menopausal women showed significant *increase in satisfaction* with their sex life.

64 percent of post-menopausal women who used supplements showed *improved sexual satisfaction* in their relationships versus only 33 percent on placebo.

Overall, 71 percent of pre- and peri-menopausal women using nutritional supplements for FSD showed an increase in desire and 68 percent an improvement in their sexual satisfaction. In the placebo group, only 49 percent reported an increase in desire and 36 percent showed improvement in sexual satisfaction.

The study concluded that herbal therapy with nutritional supplemental enhancement has a significantly positive effect on female sexual satisfaction amongst women of *all ages*, especially those in the pre- and peri-menopausal range.

◆ ◆ ◆

Another randomized double-blind study with placebo of post-menopausal women was presented at the same meeting. It looked at the effects of the oral nitric oxide precursor L-arginine and alpha-2 blocker yohimbine on sexual dysfunction in post-menopausal women. The study consisted of both subjective and objective measures, including specific physiologic testing in post-menopausal women with female sexual arousal disorder.

Oral administration of L-arginine and yohimbine had already been shown to be effective in men (versus yohimbine given alone) in increasing penile blood flow and improving erections for those with ED. Consequently, this study looked at the effects on *female* SD with doses of 6 grams of L-arginine glutamate and 6 milligrams of yohimbine hydrochloride versus yohimbine alone and placebo.

During the study, each woman was assessed at 90 minutes after the drug or placebo was administered. Physiological testing was done to measure changes in responses to sexual stimulation. Sexual arousal was further measured using a questionnaire.

The results showed the combined oral administration of L-arginine glutamate and yohimbine gave a rapid increase in sexual stimulation and function, while there was no significant increase with yohimbine alone or placebo.

These findings were consistent with previous studies showing that L-arginine combined with yohimbine has a positive effect on sexual function after about 40 minutes from administration.

This study concluded that an oral-administered combination of L-arginine and yohimbine significantly increased the general and visual female sexual arousal responses especially in post-menopausal women.

◆ ◆ ◆

A third scientific study presented at the International Female Sexual Dysfunction Meeting evaluated the effectiveness and safety of herbal therapy in the enhancement of female sexual function. This was a prospective randomized double-blind placebo controlled study of 60 women. It included quality of life information and female sexual function index questionnaires up to 3 months post-treatment on the side-effects of the herbals.

The average age of the women in this study was 46 with a range of from 22 to 67. Their education ran the gamut from high school grads to post graduate college degrees. They were from all socio-economic classes. The women had various significant symptoms of FSD and multiple risk factors for sexual dysfunction including cardiac disease, hypertension, smoking, increased age, diabetes, and caffeine consumption.

Significant improvements in sexual function were noted within one month of the study in response to key questions such as "ability to become sexually aroused" in those women taking the herbal product versus the placebo. They showed increased arousal, lubrication, and satisfaction with sexual intercourse. These trends continued up to three months.

The study concluded that sexual function in women increased and improved while continuing the therapy with the herbal supplement because it enhanced blood flow to the genitalia, and that herbal therapy may well be a *safe treatment* for women who suffer from various forms of sexual dysfunction.

◆ ◆ ◆

A fourth study presented from New York dealt with topical herbal therapy for women who have sexual dysfunction. The women tested used a vaginal lubricant applied just prior to sexual activity up to once a day. They were studied at the base line and over a two-month period using the Female Sexual Function Index, a validated questionnaire.

Women participating in this trial had sexual dysfunction and risk factors including hypertension and/or diabetes. They were often on hormone replacement therapy. Most had prior complaints of decreased arousal and difficulty achieving orgasm.

After one-month of therapy, sexual responses, including lubrication, clitoral sensation and ability to have orgasm all improved compared to their baseline.

The study concluded that vaginal lubricants safely improve women's sexual function by increasing genital blood flow, especially during short-term follow-up. Topical gels and creams that offer *immediate* stimulation may allow for effective treatment for women who have SD.

These controlled scientific studies among others support the use of herbal nutraceuticals and other dietary supplements for the treatment of sexual dysfunction in women.

◆ ◆ ◆

In May 2001, a study headed by Mary Lake Polan, MD, PHD, MPH, Professor and Chair of Gynecology and Obstetrics at Stanford University appeared in the *Journal of Woman's Health and Gender-Based Medicine.* The double-blind study concluded that a nutritional supplement was shown to significantly improve women's sexual desire and overall satisfaction.

Ninety-three women between 22 and 73-years old who said they lacked sexual desire participated in the study. 46 received the supplement and 47 got the placebo. After 4 weeks, 62 percent taking the supplement reported greater satisfaction with their total sex life compared with 38 percent in the placebo group. 64 percent of those receiving the supplement reported improvement in their sexual desire compared with 43 percent of those taking the placebo. Amongst the women who were approaching menopause, 91 percent reported more frequent intercourse as compared with 20 percent in the placebo group. The volunteers also reported no adverse effects.

The supplement contained ginkgo, ginseng, L-arginine, Damiana and 14 other vitamins and minerals. As described earlier but bears repeating, L-arginine increases levels of nitric oxide in the body, which can increase blood flow and act as a "signal" for sexual arousal.

FIFTY-FOUR

Herbals And MED

Several natural products are believed by some to help men cope with their ED. Several have been already mentioned such as: Yohimbine, L-arginine, Vitamin E, Ginger Root, Ginkgo Biloba, Korean Ginseng, Oats, Muira Puama, and Saw Palmetto.

As men age, testosterone can become increasingly bound to various proteins in the body, making it unavailable for use. Specifically, "free" or active testosterone becomes bound to albumin or sex hormone binding globulin (SHBG). As a result, less bioavailable testosterone is obtainable for the body to use.

Avena Sativa is an herbal product touted by some to help in freeing-up testosterone and creating more bioavailable testosterone to assist in improving sexual function. Avena Sativa has no known side-effects.

Similarly, **Stinging Nettles** (also known as "Nettles"), a perennial plant which grows worldwide, has been reported to block the process of testosterone being bound via SHBG and to increase sex drive. Nettles has no known side-effects.

Smilax Officinalis is a plant sterol that has been reported to boost the body's natural production of testosterone, thereby increasing energy and endurance, as well as helping to balance cholesterol. This plant also gives us the flavor called sarsaparilla.

Cholestatin is a natural product that contains the plant sterol known as beta-sitosterol. It has been purported to help maintain healthy cholesterol levels by blocking the absorption of cholesterol up to 70 percent. In addition the sterols may help increase testosterone levels in the body.

Orchic Tissue is testicular tissue obtained from various animals such as pigs (e.g. Bovine Orchic Tissue) and is a concentrated source of natural testosterone. "Denver Oysters" or pickled bull testicles were purportedly eaten by cowboys in the old west to enhance their masculinity.

Zinc is an essential mineral that may support prostate health and sexual well-being by promoting the production of testosterone. An aphrodisiac according to popular culture, oysters are said to be loaded with zinc.

Other alleged male sexual enhancers, in many cases the same as for women, include **Niacin, Rhodiola, Selenium, and Pycnogenol**, a potent antioxidant.

PART VII

PRESCRIPTION FOR SEXUAL HEALTH

23. Dr. Hakim's Office

*Dr. Hakim was pleased to observe that Elizabeth and Brad
sat closer together than most couples in the chairs opposite his
desk. A good sign.*

*"The first thing I want to tell you both is that any form of
sexual dysfunction, mild to extreme, is a couple's problem, and
that's how I prefer to treat it."*

*"You mean," Elizabeth said, "if we want to sustain our mean-
ingful relationship, we have to get back on track with each other."*

"In so many words, yes."

"What do you recommend?"

*"Brad's physical exam was completely normal. Yours too. As
I told Brad, the size of his penis is normal, and I would certainly caution against any type of enlargement surgery. His lab
tests and penile blood flow test were also pretty much normal, so
we can rule out any serious organic problems. You both need to
have a serious discussion about your feelings and desires regarding sex, and think about ways to reduce your stress and
anxiety levels. I might suggest couple counseling, perhaps even
sex therapy."*

"A shrink?"

*"A licensed sex therapist or psychologist, Brad. In the mean-
time, you and Elizabeth might want to have a long private talk
with each other. Remember, open, honest communication is the
first step to any real cure. As we talked about, there are a number of steps I have found to be helpful that can improve communication among couples, improve their sexual relations, and
ultimately their relationship as a whole. I'm going to give you
an outline of those steps to help you get started. I'll also provide*

you with a list of various herbal products that may be useful for both of you."

Dr. Hakim reached into his drawer and took out a small package containing three blue pills. "If the herbals don't help you, Brad, I want you to try one of these Viagra pills. Remember to use them as we discussed and that they require sexual stimulation to be effective. I'll give you a prescription as well."

"I thought pills were only for geezers who can't ever get it up," Brad said.

"Although your physical examination was normal, you are certainly experiencing real ED symptoms. Young couples today are often so focused on building their careers, that the stress can affect their sexual intimacy. Once you reach your 30's, especially if your nighttime or morning erections are affected, and you and your partner are experiencing sexual difficulties which are impacting your relationship as a whole, it's time to do something about it. For the time being, these pills may help. Also, by following the plan that I outlined to you, including open, honest communication with each other and working with sex therapist I recommended, you should find that your intimacy and sexual function will return in no time."

FIFTY-FIVE

I.N.T.I.M.A.C.Y.™
My 8-Step Couple's Relationship Enhancement Program

As we have seen, a number of effective methods can improve your sexual function, increase your libido, and restore the enjoyment of renewed sexual stamina. Any successful and comprehensive relationship enhancement program, however, depends upon a number of factors, including improvement of the physical, as well as the mental or emotional aspects of lovemaking in the couple. Only then can true success be achieved.

Unfortunately for many people (and it is all too common as I have seen first hand in my practice) sexual dysfunction and its related issues can *destroy* a couple's relationship and even break up otherwise happy marriages. Yes, it's true that we are sexual beings. For both women *and* men, a healthy sexual relationship is an important part of life and an important aspect of a relationship with a spouse or long-term partner.

In order to make my Relationship Enhancement Program more understandable and enjoyable, I have broken it down into 8 simple steps, which I refer to as: **I.N.T.I.M.A.C.Y.**™ and is illustrated in the table below. By following these 8 simple steps you and your partner can enjoy improved sexual health and achieve a closer, more open and honest sexual relationship. It can be easily implemented, both individually and as a couple. In this way, we can make great strides in improving the ability of couples to communicate, avoid divorce and ultimately stay together longer, and truly live happily ever after.

STEP 1: IDENTIFICATION!

First and foremost, the problem needs to be *identified* and recognized by the couple, most importantly to *themselves.* As we have discussed, almost 1 out of 2 people in the world will suffer from some form of sexual dysfunction during their lifetime. It can affect women and men

---

I.N.T.I.M.A.C.Y.™

AN 8-STEP COUPLE'S RELATIONSHIP ENHANCEMENT PROGRAM:

I:	**Identification** (Recognize you have a problem)
N:	**Notification** (Notify your partner and physician)
T:	**Thorough Examination** (See physician and follow advice)
I:	**Incorporate Lifestyle Changes**
M:	**Medical and Surgical Management**
A:	**Alternative Therapies**
C:	**Communication with your partner**
Y:	**Youthful Rejuvenation**

---

of all ages, leading to personal distress, depression and destruction of relationships.

The good news is in almost every case the problem can be successfully treated. The only caveat is that *you* need to take the first step. Once you and your partner have *identified* the problem, you then need to do something about it. Of course, it is not always easy to admit you have a problem, but once you do, the most difficult part is over. From then on, it gets easier. Why? Because a cure can be found!

STEP 2: NOTIFICATION!

Once you have *identified* the problem, the next step is *notification*. One of the unfortunate circumstances I see day after day in my practice is that both men and women all too often *wait* and *suffer in silence* with their sexual dysfunction, sometimes for *years* before seeking help and *notifying* their physician. Often, this can be traced directly to a failure to communicate their sexual problems with their partner and their physicians. Unfortunately, not all health care professionals are experts in the field of sexual health in women and men, and many, as human beings, are often uncomfortable discussing these issues. Remember, it is up to *you* to bring it up and *notify* your physician or health care provider if they do not ask you about your sexual health.

STEP 3: THOROUGH EXAMINATION

Once you have identified the problem, and notified your partner and your health care provider, you will need a *thorough examination* by your primary care physician, with appropriate referral to a medical expert if necessary for specific organic problems. You will need assurance that you have no uncontrolled chronic medical disease that may present itself *first* as *sexual dysfunction,* such as diabetes, hypertension, heart disease, atherosclerosis, or cholesterol problems, to name a few.

Today, a number of physicians specialize in the diagnosis and treatment of women and men with sexual dysfunction. Typically, a gynecologist or urologist, working together with a psychologist/sex therapist, will be able to help you and your partner understand the cause of the problem and then offer you a solution.

As discussed in earlier chapters, your physician will take a complete medical history, perform a physical examination, and order specialized laboratory tests including a complete hormonal panel. A detailed sexual history, including validated questionnaires, is extremely helpful in defining the problem. Certain routine tests may also be done, such as a Pap smear in women or a PSA blood test in men over 50 if one has not been recently performed. Various physiologic tests, such as a Duplex ultrasound or other tests of arousal may be useful in helping to make a correct diagnosis.

To reiterate, it is not uncommon that previously unknown systemic problems, including diabetes, high cholesterol or hypertension are identified during this workup, as sexual dysfunction is often the first sign of other chronic illnesses.

STEP 4: INCORPORATE LIFESTYLE CHANGES!

A number of potentially reversible lifestyle issues can negatively impact your sexual function. These include poor diet, cigarette smoking, alcohol abuse, uncontrolled stress and lack of exercise.

Patients always are asking me if certain exercises or foods improve their sex life. I tell them, *"Anything** that makes you healthier will improve your sex life!" I put an asterisk next to "anything" because certain forms of exercise or sports activities can worsen sexual function in women and men.

Although bike riding has certain aerobic benefits, clearly severe risks accompany those benefits. Vascular and neurologic injury to the delicate blood vessels and nerves of erection in men and sexual response in women can develop from traumatic compression of these tissues against the hard and unrelenting crossbar or unpadded narrow saddles so common on today's women's and men's bicycles. Let the buyer beware! If you can't give it up, look for those ergonomic bike seats now on the market. Substitute them immediately for genital friendly biking.

With regard to diet and exercise, a healthy low fat, low carbohydrate diet when combined with reasonable amounts of aerobic exercise (such as walking or making love) will contribute to a feeling of physical and mental well-being and improved sexual stamina.

Stress is a major factor that can adversely affect sexual function and normal health in general. Whether caused by job, children, money, sexual problems or other family issues, stressors can make sex more difficult, less enjoyable, and less desirable. Each partner should take an honest approach to the cause of the stress and then try to end or alleviate it. This is the most effective long-term way to manage stress successfully and thereby eliminate it as a cause of sexual dysfunction.

Similarly, avoidance of drugs and cigarette smoking are important lifestyle changes that all of us should embrace. Clearly, these factors are key in causing sexual dysfunction, and decreasing sexual stamina.

If you smoke cigarettes, stop. If you can't do it yourself, get help. A number of effective aids are out there today to help you kick the habit. By the way, all of those commercials showing lung cancer victims don't always stop cigarette smokers from smoking. However, if men in particular were to realize that each time they smoke a cigarette, *their penis shrinks*, maybe they'd finally quit! Surprise! Surprise! Maybe the Surgeon General should add "that" to the warning.

Likewise, decreasing your intake of alcohol (especially prior to sexual activity) also helps to improve sexual well-being and stamina. Remember, moderation is always the best medicine!

STEP 5: MEDICAL AND SURGICAL MANAGEMENT!

If your doctor finds anything on your evaluation that may adversely affect your overall health — especially systemic risk factors, such as diabetes, high cholesterol, high blood pressure or heart disease — it is of the utmost importance to have these problems *medically managed* properly. Again, while certain prescription medications (such as antihypertensive agents, etc.) may contribute to sexual dysfunction, these potentially serious medical problems must first be controlled. After that, the FSD or MED can often be simply and successfully treated.

Similarly, if a life-threatening illness or cancer is detected and the therapy may lead to a decrease in sexual function, bear in mind the *primary* goal is to successfully treat the illness or remove the tumor. All too often, I have seen patients avoid a potentially life saving surgery for prostate cancer due to fear of losing their ability to have an erection. Once you have been treated successfully, your sexual function can easily be fixed, but only if you are still around to enjoy it.

Specifically regarding sexual dysfunction, once a problem has been identified and the proper work-up completed, *fix it*! No valid reason in the 21st century exists to not treat sexual dysfunction.

As you have now seen, a plethora of successful *medical and surgical management* options are out there for you. The key issue to remember is no *single* treatment is right for everyone. Each person needs to be addressed as an *individual*. You need to find that treatment which is *best* for you and your partner, for your specific situation.

As I always tell my patients and their partners, you have to be happy with the treatment option that is recommended or you won't use it. Unlike treatment for a life-threatening disease or cancer, if you and your spouse/partner are not comfortable with a treatment option (like sticking a needle in your penis), or are unhappy with the outcome, side-effects or lack of spontaneity of a specific treatment, you probably won't use it! This doesn't help anybody. Therefore, you, and your partner, with the help of a qualified physician, need to find the best and most effective treatment for *both of you* as a *couple*.

STEP 6: ALTERNATIVE THERAPIES!

Much attention has been given recently to Complementary and Alternative Medicine, and the use of various natural and herbal **alternative therapies** for the treatment of sexual dysfunction in women and men. While I honestly feel these treatments will often be less than optimal for those with severe organic sexual dysfunction, millions of women and men in the world with less severe sexual dysfunction may respond favorably to lifestyle changes (e.g. improved communication, stopping smoking, decreasing alcohol intake, stress reduction, etc.) coupled with alternative therapies, which may improve sexual and overall health.

For example, Dr. Irwin Goldstein, the world-renowned SD researcher, has demonstrated convincingly that DHEA, a nutraceutical supplement available in most health food stores without a prescription, may in fact be *the* "magic pill" for many women with sexual dysfunction.

In addition, numerous researchers and medical practitioners have seen the beneficial results of other specific nutritional supplements in the treatment of their patients with various medical problems, such as prostatitis (Prosta-Q), benign prostatic hypertrophy or BPH (Saw Palmetto), prostate cancer (PC-Spes), and cystitis (Cysta-Q).

Recent scientific papers presented at International Meetings have demonstrated significant improvement in Female Sexual Arousal Disorder and other forms of female and male sexual dysfunction using herbal supplements. I recommend a healthy lifestyle, excellent communication, good nutrition, moderate exercise and the use of various nutritional and herbal supplements on a regular basis to help *support* good health and normal sexual function, even as early as your 20's and 30's. In fact, this may be a simple and effective way to *prevent* or *delay* the onset of sexual dysfunction in women and men.

I believe if you can do this, from young adulthood through old age, you can continue to enjoy a wonderful sex-life together. Then, if a more severe organic sexual problem does develop, the sexually happy and aware couple will be ready and willing to find a cure as soon as possible, in order to *maintain* their shared intimacy and quality of life.

STEP 7: COMMUNICATION WITH YOUR PARTNER!

One major reason why couples do not experience optimal sexual pleasure in their relationship can be traced directly to a *failure to communicate*. As a result, frustration develops, tensions worsen, and the intimacy ends, all of which can often be easily prevented simply by *talking* to one another.

Yes, I know *communication with your partner* is not always as simple as it sounds. It's not always easy to tell your spouse what you like, what you want them to do, or what displeases you — but the alternative should be unacceptable. Lack of communication leads to increased stress in the relationship and makes all other couple issues even more difficult to deal with. This can cause a vicious cycle or "Catch-22", whereby the couple, like partners in a business, becomes distant or estranged.

What do I recommend? Simple. Talk to each other. Put aside a few minutes each day alone with your lover and express your feelings. Unless you and your partner communicate your likes and dislikes with regard to lovemaking, you won't be able to achieve the ultimate in sexual pleasure. And remember, it doesn't have to be negative. If you really like what they did to you the last time you had sex, tell them!

Don't be shy when talking to your partner about what you like or don't like, or how you like to be pleased sexually. You both want to achieve maximum pleasure from sexual activity, and only open communication and honesty can get you there.

Also, I sincerely believe if you are going to tell your lover something "negative" or something they may take in a harmful manner, despite your honesty, use discretion. The time *never* to critique your partner is in the bedroom immediately before, during or after sex. Egos can be fragile, and sometimes even a simple criticism can be taken the wrong way. Instead, talk to your partner honestly, in a non-threatening situation, and with some delicacy. One word of caution, if possible, always make it a "positive" experience, by combining a criticism with a compliment, for instance by telling your spouse "It feels so nice when you're making love to me ... I bet it would also feel amazing if you were to use your hands and tongue on me, like this ..."

Don't only *tell* your lover what you want, *show them*. Use your hands, tongue, lips, or toys to illustrate your desires. Caress yourself where and how you enjoy being touched. This can make a much greater impact and reinforce your comfort with your own body as well.

STEP 8: YOUTHFUL REJUVENATION!

Sometimes, identification, notification, lifestyle changes and even medical management by themselves, may not be enough to renew your intimacy. Most busy adults face the normal stressors and responsibilities of daily life. Between family, children, job and other activities, it's generally difficult to sit down for 5 minutes and breathe, let alone find time for communication and intimacy or to even *think* about *sex*. This isn't healthy for your relationship as a couple and often leads to increased stress and personal distress. To *regain* that initial thrill and *lost intimacy* of your relationship, you and your partner need to make a commitment to change and new ideas, or as I like to call it: *youthful rejuvenation.*

In order for you and your partner to maximally enjoy enhanced sexual intimacy, you have to be "on the same page." For one thing, you both need to be "in the mood," hopefully at the same time. Unfortunately, if you always wait for "spontaneous sex," until you're both sexually aroused, you and your spouse will probably make love much less often, which can adversely affect your relationship.

Often the most effective methods to get "on the same page" sexually and improve "spontaneity" are to focus on your *partner's* desires or needs. What gets *them* aroused? What gets *them* sexually excited? By asking yourself and your spouse these questions and doing whatever it takes for arousal, you can help to bring your partner to an enhanced level of sexual desire.

The idea of "spontaneity" with regard to lovemaking and couple's intimacy is actually something of a misnomer. Sure, it's wonderful to surprise your partner once in a while to spice up your lovemaking. Spur-of-the-moment sex or a "quickie" with your spouse can be a wonderful and exciting pleasure, but couples can't always count on this to happen. Remember, *opportunity comes to those who are ready for it.* So, why wait for spontaneous sex to just happen? Chances are that it probably won't, or if it does, not all that frequently.

You ask, "What can I do to improve our intimacy and achieve that *youthful rejuvenation?*" One thing you can do is *make a date* with your partner/spouse at least once a week. Plan a romantic evening alone with your lover. Hire a babysitter or arrange for the kids to stay with grandma. Whether you go to a fancy restaurant, or spend a cozy evening alone at home, it doesn't really matter. The most important thing is that both of you have an opportunity to spend quality time together.

Talk to each other, not about daily life stress or work, but about your love for each other. Do not forget what brought you together in the first place. How you first fell in love with each other. Talk about the future. Talk about your desires and most importantly *relax together*, with candles, a glass of wine (not a bottle ... also remember, alcohol deadens the sexual response), maybe a warm bath ... a sensual massage ... all of the things that make life worth living together.

One of the frequent issues I see in my practice with regard to improving a couple's intimacy is often times, they may not even know what *really* excites their partners. Of course, the solution to this problem can often be summed up in a single word: *communication*! However, if you and your partner agree this is the problem, based on my experience, I can suggest a number of things you can do together to increase intimacy, improve quality time and enhance your sexual relationship.

Sensual Massage: A sensual massage is a great way to help your partner relax and "get in the mood". And you don't have to be a professional masseur or masseuse for it to be pleasurable. Gentle touching of your partner, in a quiet, relaxed and peaceful setting (e.g. No Kids!) can be enough for many couples to establish a heightened level of sexual arousal.

Tantalize your Partner: Foreplay, fiveplay, sixplay! You and your partner can heighten each other's level of arousal by tantalizing and teasing each other. Instead of just doing the routine, and heading straight for intercourse, both sexes should concentrate at first on erogenous zones such as the nipples, nape of the neck, shoulders, back and thighs. And ladies, men will love these same techniques, too.

The *key* is to touch each other gently, slowly and softly, heightening pleasure by coming as close to the erogenous zones as possible, without directly stimulating them. Remember, ask your partner what feels good. By taking your time, you can enjoy incredible levels of sexual pleasure together, even before the "main event".

Try New Positions: Many couples fall into a rut, and deprive themselves of new sensations and experiences by following the same routine every time they make love. Why not experiment with new positions? If you and your lover always have sex in the missionary position, how about trying the "woman on top" position. This allows her to control the level of penetration and achieve more stimulation of the clitoris during intercourse. She can also sit back and caress and stimulate herself, while arousing her partner at the same time.

Kneeling, with the women on her hands and knees, while the man penetrates her vagina from behind allows for deeper penetration, while leaving his hands free to caress her breasts, back and other erogenous areas.

Side-by-side lovemaking or the couple lying on their sides with the man behind his partner, are variations that allow for different sensations and exciting possibilities.

Couples who openly communicate can select from any number of positions and experiment in order to add variety and spice to their lovemaking. These varying positions can further increase sexual satisfaction and are only limited by your imagination.

Also, try changing locations. If you and your spouse always have sex in the bedroom, do it in the kitchen, the shower, the beach, or even the car, for those seeking that added thrill of "the potential of getting caught"!

Excite with your Tongue: Although taboo in certain cultures, oral stimulation of the erogenous zones and genitals can be extremely erotic for both female and male. Using your lips and tongue to stimulate your lover can lead to intensely arousing sensations. Unlike manual stimulation with your fingers and hands, which is also quite erotic, the warmth and wetness of oral stimulation offers new heights of arousal for your partner especially as a means of foreplay. Oral sex also includes "talking explicitly" or describing in detail during sexual activity what you want or need.

The only rules are to have enjoyment, and do whatever is desired to stimulate and excite your lover. By doing this, the unselfish lover quickly realizes it can be just as arousing to give oral sex, as it is to receive it.

Sex Toys: *If* each partner is willing and open to it, sex toys can offer an exciting dimension to sexual activity. Various *toys* for couples can intensify the pleasure you are giving and receiving during lovemaking. From a simple feather, to a vibrator, to a blindfold, to fur-lined cuffs, sex toys can escalate the level of fantasy and arousal, providing pleasure, unique sensations, new heights of ecstasy and experiences to both lovers.

Again, as long as both partners consent, the only rules are to be creative and have fun. Open and honest communication is critical for both women and men to achieve their greatest sexual fantasies and pleasure. The more you can try new things to please each other, the greater the level of arousal and passion you will achieve. Ultimately, your relationship will continue to grow and flourish. By following the steps above, you'll both be ready for a life of incredible sexual pleasure, enhanced intimacy and *youthful rejuvenation.*

Remember, always use your imagination and think of new ways to pleasure your lover. The only goal should be for both of you to have fun, increase both of your sexual pleasures, and enable you and your lover to achieve sexual nirvana.

◆ ◆ ◆

If every couple could follow these 8 simple steps, how great their lives together might be. I truly feel that the I.N.T.I.M.A.C.Y.™ program will serve to enhance relationships, keep love lives fresh and bring couples closer together. Yes, the I.N.T.I.M.A.C.Y.™ program will allow you to achieve and sustain new, higher levels of happiness and sexual bliss.

Not a bad goal is it to find solutions that help us live and love better, happily ever after?

24. Dr. Hakim's Office

After Dr. Hakim finished with his last patient of the day, he took time out to read his mail before going home to his beautiful wife and kids. One letter was from Elizabeth.

Dear Dr. Hakim,

How are you? We are fine, better than we have been in months. After our visit with you, Brad and I had a very long talk. We agreed that we were both exhausted after we got home at night, and that making love had become an obligatory chore. The sex therapist you recommended also was helpful. She really listened to us and made some fabulous suggestions.

We then read through your 8-step plan and decided to take your advice and go away for a quiet weekend. We agreed to abide by two rules. Forget our work and relax.

We spent the weekend at a beach resort in the Keys. Brad tried the Viagra you gave him. Whether it was that little blue pill or simply unstressing ourselves and reaffirming our love for each other ... well, let me put it this way. We made love more than a few times, and it was great! And Brad did not even need Viagra after the first day.

We look forward to seeing you again when it is time for our next physicals.

Oh, yes, one more thing. I went cold turkey. No more cigarettes! Thank you for your great advice and kindness.

Sincerely,

Elizabeth and Brad

Dr. Hakim smiled. Brad had signed it, rather boldly too. No problem, it seemed, with his testosterone.

Appendix A: Sexually Transmitted Diseases

If you accept that sexual dysfunction is a couple's disease, then we are obligated to include other couple's diseases here as a public service and, yes, as a warning.

The incidence of sexually transmitted diseases (STDs) has dramatically increased over the past 30 years. STDs, at one time more commonly called VD (venereal disease), can cause sexual dysfunction in both women and men. STDs are most common in young, sexually active women and men, and the incidence does decrease with age. However, as a result of the Baby Boomers, born in the decade after WWII, this sexually active group has been growing in numbers.

Many STDs, especially AIDS (Acquired Immunodeficiency Syndrome) are spreading at such an alarming rate that sexually active women and men have just cause for panic. Incredibly, high-risk behavior in certain populations continues to increase! STDs can ruin a person's health, infect others, destroy marriages and relationships, and may even lead to death.

STDs are becoming more frequent in women. Growing numbers of women are having sex at a younger age, and the number of partners they are likely to have has grown far beyond what it was before the 1960s. This has resulted in a proportional growth in STDs amongst women, along with the serious consequences of promiscuity, such as pelvic inflammatory disease (PID) and infertility.

Women are more susceptible to infection than men. "STDs are inherently sexist," says Dr. H. Hunter Handsfield, professor of medicine at the University of Washington and director of Seattle and King County's STD Control Program. The skin of the male penis is more resistant to pathogens than the female's vagina and cervix. Women run the risk of infertility, as well. Some of the most tragic consequences of STDs in women include ectopic pregnancies (outside the uterus) and cervical carcinoma, and may occur years after initial exposure. Men are more likely to infect women than the other way around.

The United States has the highest rate of STD in the industrialized world. Conservatively, we have more than 15-million new cases every year. ASHA, the American Social Health Association estimates this breakdown of *new* incidences each year as follows:

STD INCIDENCE	
Chlamydia	3 million
Gonorrhea	650,000
Syphilis	70,000
Herpes	1 million
HPV	5.5 million
Hepatitis B	77,000
Trichomoniasis	5 million
HIV	20,000

You should know the symptoms of each infection and perform regular self-examinations, especially if you are not in a healthy long-term monogamous relationship and instead are sexually active with many partners. In the following pages, we will discuss some of the more common STDs, although it is certainly not meant to be an inclusive and exhaustive list. Evaluation by a qualified physician is critical if you suspect you or your partner has one of the STDs.

URETHRITIS (GONOCOCCAL AND NON-GONOCOCCAL URETHRITIS):

Gonorrhea remains the most commonly reported communicable disease in the United States. Gonococcal urethritis (Gonorrhea) is associated with the gram-negative bacteria *N. gonorrhea*. Although GU is usually contracted during intercourse, infection may be transmitted through oral sex as well, and the risk increases as the number of sexual partners increases. The incubation period is 3-10 days, but exceptions are common.

Unfortunately, after 12 years of decline, gonorrhea rates have risen in the United States, to 8 times that of Canada, and 50 times that of Sweden.

Approximately 25 percent of new cases reported each year are in teenagers.

Classically, GU causes burning during urination and pus-like discharge from the vagina or urethra, often profuse, but sometimes scant. GU may be symptomatic in 40-60 percent of the contacts of partners with known gonorrhea! It may also lead to pelvic inflammatory disease and infertility. As with syphilis, it facilitates the transmission of HIV.

The diagnosis of GU is made clinically in a laboratory with culture of urethral swabs of the infected area. If there is a history of oral genital contact, throat cultures may be necessary.

GU may be successfully treated by a physician once a diagnosis is made. Appropriate antibiotics and continued condom usage, along with partner screening and treatment are essential for a successful outcome.

One cause of the rise of gonorrhea is the appearance of drug-resistant strains. Penicillin and tetracycline have not been as effective since the 1980s. Epidemiologists are now seeing equal resistance in the United States to newer antibiotics. However, thanks to recent publicity, there is hope that rates have started to drop again.

CHLAMYDIA:

NGU surpasses gonorrhea as the more common diagnosis for patient visits to doctors' offices (2.5 x GU!). NGU is a syndrome with several causes. The most important pathogen, which accounts for 30-50 percent of cases, is Chlamydia (*C. trachomatis*), although the organism Ureaplasma accounts for 20 percent of cases. The incubation period for NGU is 1-5 weeks, but can be longer.

Chlamydia is a bacterial infection that can lurk in a woman's reproductive system. When symptoms do occur, they include a mucous discharge that some can mistake as a yeast infection, burning during urination, or some spotting after sexual intercourse. Women should know that if they do not treat chlamydia, it can cause pelvic inflammatory disease and scarring that can block their fallopian tubes causing infertility. It can easily be treated in a short time with antibiotics if the STD is discovered early.

In men, symptoms usually involve painful urination or *dysuria* and urethral discharge. Diagnosis of NGU requires demonstration of urethritis with exclusion of gonorrhea. Urethral discharge is usually scant, and asymptomatic infection is common.

Like gonorrhea, NGU may be successfully treated by a physician once a diagnosis is made. Appropriate antibiotics and continued condom usage along with partner screening and treatment are necessary for a successful outcome.

While gonorrhea and NGU may be prevented by regular use of condoms, the best defense against any STD begins with abstinence and education, and continues with safe sex.

EPIDIDYMITIS:

Acute epididymitis is a syndrome resulting from pain, inflammation, and swelling of the epididymis, the organ attached to the testicle. Complications can include pain and infertility. The cause is frequently due to STDs in young, sexually active men. Chlamydia accounts for most of those cases, although other organisms can be the culprit. The diagnosis is made by patient history and a physical exam by a physician, and must be differentiated from *testicular torsion*, an emergency condition involving twisting of the spermatic cord and testicle with loss of blood flow, especially in young men.

Treatment of acute epididymitis involves a combination of specific antibiotics, anti-inflammatory agents, bed rest, avoidance of strenuous activity or heavy lifting, scrotal elevation, and warm compresses as needed.

GENITAL HERPES INFECTIONS:

Genital herpes simplex virus (HSV) is a disease of great concern to all, with an increasing incidence and high morbidity. HSV-II is usually associated with genital herpes. Type I herpes, HSV-1, is commonly associated with oral infections, causing sores to develop around the mouth that may be transmitted to the partner's genital region through oral sex. In college students, HSV infection is 10 times more common than gonorrhea or syphilis. Partners are at risk even when the infection is asymptomatic, although the risk of transmission is certainly lower when couples avoid contact during clinical outbreaks.

The diagnosis is made by identification of small vesicles on a reddish base. The clusters of small ulcers are filled with clear fluid that crust over and heal within days and confirmation is based on laboratory methods.

Effective treatment with antiviral therapy, such as Acyclovir® or Penciclovir®, is available from a physician once a diagnosis is made. Oral Acyclovir and other antiviral therapies are effective in treating recurrent genital herpes infections.

Estimates are that 45-million Americans (one in six) are currently affected, with a million new cases reported each year. Many women are unaware they may have herpes and assume they're experiencing minor itching or sores on their genitalia. Aside from the discomfort and embarrassment of repeated flare-ups, major problems can occur if a woman develops an infection during the third trimester of pregnancy and exposes her baby to lesions in the birth canal.

GENITAL WARTS:

"Some experts think that 70 percent of all adults may acquire a HPV (Human Papilloma Virus) infection at some time in their life. It may resolve itself, but we don't really know if it goes away entirely." So said Dr. Peter Leone, assistant professor of medicine at the University of North Carolina and medical director of the Wade County STD, HIV, and TB programs.

Transmission of the disease occurs when the released viral particles from the lesions come in contact with another person. Men infected with HPV are carriers and generally show no symptoms. Only about 1 percent develops genital warts. Some strains of the virus can be associated with cancer of the penis and anal area.

Although the majority of HPV infections are benign, researchers have established a link between some strains of the virus and cervical cancer in women. About 80 strains of the virus are known. Types 16, 18, 31, 33, and 35 have been strongly associated with cervical dysplasia (abnormal growths) in women and the development of cancer. Types 6 and 11 are often most responsible for genital warts. The lesions can disappear after several months or linger for many years, which is why women *must* undergo a Pap smear each year.

Male partners of these infected women must go to their urologists and confirm if they indeed carry the virus.

The goal of treatment is removal of visible warts. Unfortunately, no treatment has been shown to completely eradicate HPV.

PRIMARY SYPHILIS:

The incidence of syphilis is now higher than it has been in the past three decades. More than 55,000 cases of syphilis were reported in 1990, the highest since 1949, with many of the increases occurring in populations with a high prevalence of HIV infection. Encouraged by reports of new effective drugs and longer life for AIDS patients, some gay and bisexual men have recently returned to unsafe anonymous sex and bathhouse encounters with little or no use of condoms. The Center for Disease Control reported that 75 percent of syphilis victims in 1999 were African-American.

Syphilis is caused by an organism known as a spirochete, Treponema pallidum, and gains access to the body through the skin or mucous membranes. The incubation period is typically 2-4 weeks, and a man who has been exposed will usually develop a painless sore called a "chancre".

The chancre begins as a small red spot or papule. It then breaks down to form a hardened, 'punched-out' lesion on the genitalia or other areas of sexual contact, such as the lips or tongue. This lesion at the site of contact often goes away in a few weeks, and may be followed by a rash and swollen glands. If left untreated, it can cause chronic illness and even death. Syphilis infections can weaken resistance to HIV infection as well.

Diagnosis is made by microscopic examination of the lesion and its fluid. Serologic or blood tests, such as VDRL and RPR tests, can help in the diagnosis.

Successful treatment of syphilis involves Benzathine® penicillin as a first line therapy. Other antibiotics may also be successful. Treatment failures may occur, however, and patients should be re-examined at 3 and 6 months. All patients with syphilis should be encouraged to be tested for HIV as well.

HIV:

So much has been written about the social and pathological causes of HIV and AIDS that the subject can only be given justice in a separate book. The best way to avoid getting this disease is to always adhere to all the principals of SAFE SEX, consider abstinence if necessary, use condoms, and avoid sharing needles.

◆ ◆ ◆

In summary, STDs are very common in sexually active people. The signs and symptoms of various STDs, including chlamydia, herpes, and HPV, are often difficult to detect, even if you regularly inspect your genitalia. Always bear in mind, *condoms may not prevent transmission of all STDs!*

Sexually active women in particular should have regularly scheduled sexual examinations by a health professional every *six months*. Some advocate self-examinations at least once a month, especially after involvement with a new partner.

Of course, the best defense against all STDs begins with abstinence and education, continues with safe sex, and hopefully concludes with a healthy, preferably lifetime monogamous partner.

Appendix B: Helpful Organizations

American Association of Sex Educators, Counselors, and Therapists (ASSECT)
PO BOX 5488
Richmond, VA 23220-0488
1-804-644-3288
Fax: 1-804-644-3290
ASSECT@mediaone.net

American Foundation for Urologic Disease
1128 North Charles Street
Baltimore, M.D. 21201
1-410-468-1808
www.impotence.org
www.afud.org

Cleveland Clinic Florida-Weston
Section, Sexual Dysfunction, Male Infertility and Prosthetics
2950 Cleveland Clinic Blvd.
Weston, Florida 33331
954-659-5188
www.sexhealthnet.com

US TOO International, Inc.
Prostate Cancer Support Groups
930 N. York Road, Suite 50
Hinsdale, IL 60521
1-800-808-7866
www.ustoo.com

Working Group For A New View Of Women's Sexual Problems
c/o Dr. Leonore Tiefer, Ph.D.
163 Third Ave PMB #183
New York, NY 10003
LTiefer@mindspring.com

OTHER HELPFUL WEBSITES:

www.thecouplesdisease.com
www.sexhealthnet.net
www.fsff.org
www.mentorcorp.com
www.visitams.com
www.intimacyplan.com

Appendix C: Recommended Reading

Books:

Goldstein, Irwin. *The Potent Male*. Regenesis Cycle Publishing Inc. 1995

Holstein, Lana L. *How to Have Magnificent Sex: The 7 Dimensions of a Vital Sexual Connection*. New York: Harmony Books, 2001.

Masters, William, Virginia Johnson, and Robert Kolodry. *Masters and Johnson on Sex & Human Loving*. Boston: Little Brown & Co., 1986.

Nickell, Nancy L. *Natures Aphrodisiacs*. California: The Crossing Press. 1999

Reichman, Judith. *I'm Not in the Mood: What Every Woman Should Know About Improving Her Libido*. New York: Quill William Morrow, 1999.

Rosen, R and Leiblum, S. *Principles and Practice of Sex Therapy*. New York: The Guilford Press, 1995.

Journal Articles:

Basson R, Berman J, Burnett A, Derogatis L, Ferguson D, Fourcroy J, Goldstein I, Graziottin A, Heiman J, Laan E, Leiblum S, Padma-Nathan H, Rosen R, Segraves K, Segraves RT, Shabsigh R, Sipski M, Wagner G, Whipple B. Report of the International Consensus Development

Conference on Female Sexual Dysfunction: definitions and classifications. Journal of Urology. 2000 Mar; 163(3):888-93

Basson, R. *Human sex-response cycles.* Journal of Sex and Marital Therapy. 2001 Jan-Feb;27(1):33-43.

Berman, J and Goldstein I. *Female sexual dysfunction.* Urologic Clinics of North America. 2001 May;28(2):405-16.

Berman, J and Goldstein I. Female sexual dysfunction: incidence, pathophysiology, evaluation, and treatment options. Urology. 1999 Sep;54(3):385-91.

Goldstein, Irwin et al. for the Sildenafil Study Group. *Oral Sildenafil in the Treatment of Erectile Dysfunction.* The New England Journal of Medicine 338(20) 1998:1397-1404.

Goldstein, I. *Female sexual arousal disorder: new insights.* International Journal of Impotence Research. 2000 Oct;12 Suppl 4:S152-7.

Hakim, LS et al. *Comparative results of goal oriented therapy for erectile dysfunction.* International Journal of Impotence Research. 1997 Sep;9(3):174-5.

Hakim, LS et al. *Fasting Lipid Values and Presence of Female Sexual Arousal Disorder in Women with no other Medical Co-morbidities.* (Submitted for publication) Endocrinology Metabolic Clinics of North America. 2002

Hakim, LS and Goldstein I. *Diabetic sexual dysfunction.* Endocrinology Metabolic Clinics of North America. 1996 Jun;25(2):379-400.

Hakim, LS, Kulaksizoglu H and Goldstein I et al. *Evolving concepts in the diagnosis and treatment of arterial high flow priapism.* Journal of Urology. 1996 Feb;155(2):541-8.

Hakim, LS and Goldstein I, et al. *Vacuum erection associated impotence and Peyronie's disease.* Journal of Urology. 1996 Feb;155(2):534-5.

Hakim, LS, Kulaksizoglu H and Goldstein I et al. *Penile microvascular arterial bypass surgery.* Microsurgery. 1995;16(5):296-308.

Laumann, EO, Paik, A and Rosen RC. *Sexual dysfunction in the United States: prevalence and predictors.* Journal of the American Medical Association. 1999 Feb 10;281 (6):537-44.

Leiblum, S. *Persistent sexual arousal syndrome: a newly discovered pattern of female sexuality.* Journal of Sex and Marital Therapy. 2001 Jul-Sep;27(4):365-80.

NIH Consensus Development Panel on Impotence. *Impotence.* Journal of the American Medical Association (JAMA). 270 (1) 1993:83-90

Rosen, R, Brown, C, Heiman, J, Leiblum, S et al. *The Female Sexual Function Index (FSFI): a multidimensional self-report instrument for the assessment of female sexual function.* Journal of Sex and Marital Therapy. 2000 Apr-Jun;26 (2):191-208.

Shifren, JL, Rosen, RC, Leblum, S et al. *Transdermal testosterone treatment in women with impaired sexual function after oophorectomy.* New England Journal of Medicine. 2000 Sep 7;343(10):682-8.

ABOUT THE AUTHOR

Born in 1962, Lawrence S. Hakim, MD, FACS currently is Head of the Section of Sexual Dysfunction, Male Infertility, and Prosthetics at the Cleveland Clinic Florida, located in Weston, Florida, where he also directs a post-graduate Fellowship Training program in Andrology. Dr. Hakim serves on advisory boards and is a consultant to a number of medical equipment and pharmaceutical companies. He is a graduate of Rensselaer Polytechnic Institute, where he received both a Bachelor's and Master's degree in Biology, and the State University of New York Downstate Medical School, from which he received his medical degree. Dr. Hakim completed a Post-Graduate Fellowship at Boston University Medical Center, with Dr. Irwin Goldstein, the "father" of modern SD research, in Sexual Dysfunction, Male Infertility, and Microsurgery. Dr. Lawrence S. Hakim has also served as Assistant Professor, University of Miami School of Medicine, Department of Urology, in Miami, Florida. He has written and published many scientific articles in the peer-reviewed literature, and has received the distinction of Diplomate of the American Board of Urology and Fellowship in the American College of Surgeons. Dr. Hakim is a frequent television and radio guest, and is a highly sought-after speaker in the area of sexual medicine and surgery, both nationally and internationally.

Donald Michael Platt has sold his fiction to film and TV and collaborated with Carl DeSantis, founder of Rexall Sundown, on his autobiography, VITAMIN EN*RICH*ED.

315

If you cannot find *The Couple's Disease* in bookstores or online, please order from:

1-800-ALL-BOOK
1-800-255-2665

For further information,
please visit our website at:
www.thecouplesdisease.com

or write to:

DHP Publishers, LLC
1730 S. Federal Highway, Suite #378
Delray Beach, FL 33483-3309